Sleeping Beauty

A Victorian Pantomime

Alan Brown

A SAMUEL FRENCH ACTING EDITION

SAMUELFRENCH-LONDON.CO.UK
SAMUELFRENCH.COM

Copyright © 1993 by Alan Brown
All Rights Reserved

SLEEPING BEAUTY is fully protected under the copyright laws of the British Commonwealth, including Canada, the United States of America, and all other countries of the Copyright Union. All rights, including professional and amateur stage productions, recitation, lecturing, public reading, motion picture, radio broadcasting, television and the rights of translation into foreign languages are strictly reserved.

ISBN 978-0-573-06491-3

www.samuelfrench-london.co.uk

www.samuelfrench.com

FOR AMATEUR PRODUCTION ENQUIRIES

UNITED KINGDOM AND WORLD EXCLUDING NORTH AMERICA

plays@SamuelFrench-London.co.uk

020 7255 4302/01

Each title is subject to availability from Samuel French, depending upon country of performance.

CAUTION: Professional and amateur producers are hereby warned that SLEEPING BEAUTY is subject to a licensing fee. Publication of this play does not imply availability for performance. Both amateurs and professionals considering a production are strongly advised to apply to the appropriate agent before starting rehearsals, advertising, or booking a theatre. A licensing fee must be paid whether the title is presented for charity or gain and whether or not admission is charged.

The professional rights in this play are controlled by Samuel French Ltd, 52 Fitzroy Street, London, W1T 5JR.

No one shall make any changes in this title for the purpose of production. No part of this book may be reproduced, stored in a retrieval system, or transmitted in any form, by any means, now known or yet to be invented, including mechanical, electronic, photocopying, recording, videotaping, or otherwise, without the prior written permission of the publisher. No one shall upload this title, or part of this title, to any social media websites.

The right of Alan Brown to be identified as author of this work has been asserted by him in accordance with Section 77 of the Copyright, Designs and Patents Act 1988

SLEEPING BEAUTY

First produced by Richard Eyre at the Playhouse Theatre, Nottingham, with the following cast:

Princess Beauty	Lynsey Baxter
King	Trevor T. Smith
Queen	Joan Heal
Nanny	Bryan Pringle
Nuts	Sarah Bennett
General Dogsbody	Sylvester McCoy
Frivolette	Anthea Ferrell
Prince Florizel	Celia Foxe
Obadiah I	Patrick McIntyre
Obadiah II	Duncan Faber
Dragon	Louisa Rix, Helen Brammer, Sheraton Blount
President	Arthur Kohn
Policeman	Roy Jones
Luna	Pat Keen
Malevola	Malcolm Storry
Imp	Duncan Faber
Father Time	Arthur Kohn
Fairies	Louisa Rix, Judy Riley, Buster Skeggs, Sarah Bennett, Sheraton Blount, Helen Brammer
Pages/Choirboys	Masters Jeremy Cornes, Adam Crevald, Andrew Crevald, Andrew Dixon, Robert Gale, Jeremy Hague, Taras Moroz, Christopher Vivian
Maids, Witches, Senators, Lackeys	Members of the Company

Director/Choreographer Gillian Lynne
Designer Tim Goodchild
Stage Manager Roy Jones

CHARACTERS

Princess Beauty
King, her father
Queen, her mother
Nanny, her nurse
Nuts, her dog
General Dogsbody, a court factotum
Frivolette, lady-in-waiting
Palace Maids, Lackeys, etc.

THE FUTURE
Prince Florizel
Obadiah I
Obadiah II
Dragon
President
Policeman
Senators, Curator, Citizens of the Future, etc.

IMMORTALS
Luna, the Moon fairy
Malevola, a wicked fairy
Imp
Father Time
Vedonia
Elegantia
Melodia } fairies
Camilla
Thalia
Pamela
Witches

HARLEQUINADE
Columbine (Princess Beauty)   **Pantaloon** (King)
Harlequin (Prince)   **Policeman** (Obadiah I)
Clown (Nurse)   **Butcher** (Dogsbody)
Parson (Obadiah II)   **Dog** (Nuts)
Nursemaid (Queen)   **Choirboys**

SYNOPSIS OF SCENES

ACT I
SCENE 1   The Abode of the Wicked Fairy
SCENE 2   The Royal Palace
SCENE 3   The Abode of Time
SCENE 4   The Royal Palace
SCENE 5   The Abode of Time
SCENE 6   A Dense Forest

ACT II
SCENE 1   The Abode of Time
SCENE 2   A Grand Corridor in the Palace
SCENE 2A Harlequinade — "Princess Beauty's Dream"
SCENE 3   Outside the Royal Palace
SCENE 4   The Palace of the New Republic
SCENE 5   Outside the National Museum
SCENE 6   The Abode of Time
SCENE 7   Princess Beauty's Wedding

PRODUCTION NOTE

During the arrival of the audience an advertisement-cloth is displayed bearing 1890s period advertisements by local shops and firms still in existence today. Immediately prior to the rise of the Curtain the advertisement-cloth is raised, and a Victorian stage manager comes from behind the curtain with a lighted taper and ignites the (imitation) footlights.

SONGS

Please remember that a licence issued by Samuel French Ltd to perform this pantomime does NOT include permission to use copyright songs and music. Please read the notice supplied by the Performing Right Society on page viii.

ACT I

Song 1	Company
Song 2	Nurse
Song 3	Malevola
Song 4	Company
Song 5	Princess
Song 6	Prince

ACT II

Song 7	Dogsbody, King, Queen, Nurse, Housemaids
Song 8	Nurse, Company
Song 9	Prince, Princess
Song 10	King, Company
Song 11	Obadiah I, Frivolette
Song 12	Princess, Prince, Nurse, King
Song 13	Princess, Dogsbody, Nurse, King, Obadiah I, Frivolette, Company
Song 14	Malevola, Luna
Song 15	(reprise of Song 13) Company

A list of suggested songs is available from Alan Brown
c/o Samuel French Ltd

The following statement concerning the use of music is printed here on behalf of the Performing Right Society Ltd, by whom it was supplied

The permission of the owner of the performing right in copyright music must be obtained before any public performance may be given, whether in conjunction with a play or sketch or otherwise, and this permission is just as necessary for amateur performances as for professional. The majority of copyright musical works (other than oratorios, musical plays and similar dramatico-musical works) are controlled in the British Commonwealth by the PERFORMING RIGHT SOCIETY LTD, 29-33 BERNERS STREET, LONDON W1P 4AA.

The Society's practice is to issue licences authorizing the use of its repertoire to the proprietors of premises at which music is publicly performed, or, alternatively, to the organizers of musical entertainments, but the Society does not require payment of fees by performers as such. Producers or promoters of play, sketches, etc., at which music is to be performed, during or after the play or sketch, should ascertain whether the premises at which their performances are to be given are covered by a licence issued by the Society, and if they are not, should make application to the Society for particulars as to the fee payable.

Other pantomimes by Alan Brown
published by Samuel French Ltd

Aladdin and his Wonderful Lamp
Babes in the Wood
Cinderella
Dick Whittington
Puss in Boots

ACT I

Scene 1

The Abode of the Wicked Fairy. Frontcloth

Music: "Walpurgisnacht" from Ballet Music to Gounod's Faust

Malevola is discovered, chained to a huge fiery rock, on the top of which is a huge hour-glass. The sand is about to run out. Thunder and lightning

Malevola	Great elements of fire! Ye all must know
	The hour has almost come for me to go.
	A thousand years have fled and found me fast
	Chained to this fiery rock for deeds long past.
	'Twas then for mystic murders I was tried,
	And to this stake, done to a steak, was tied.
	Of course, a punishment like that to me
	Is but a trifle, and when I'm set free
	You'll find again for mischief I am game:
	I'll do ... I'll do ... a deed without a name!

(She shrieks with laughter)

The Imp enters and falls to his knees

	So, Imp! My time is nearly up. What's new?
Imp	Malevola — Have I got news for you!
	The king's to give a banquet and a ball —
	And all the world's invited, great and small —
	In honour of the birth of a princess,
	But you're not likely to be there, I guess.
	The other Fairies are — *they*'ve been invited ——
Malevola	Invited! Fairies? — And me slighted?
	I've had no invitation! Did they dare
	Accept without me? But I shall be there!

> I'll have revenge for all my suffering strange.
> As for this sovereign, him I'll quickly change;
> For I shall go and give him tit for tat,
> And squeeze the life out of his precious brat!

The hour-glass gives off a spark and a small puff of smoke as the last grain drops. There is a roll of thunder. A large flash and another puff of smoke and Malevola's chains break asunder. A harvest moon appears at the back

> Ha! Free once more! Now they shall feel my power!
> Away! And meet me at the Palace Tower!

The Imp exits

> The Moon is up, the mist is on the brae,
> The spirit of Mac — but enough! Away!

The Moon opens disclosing the Fairy Luna

Luna   Stop! I command you. I have heard the threat
Of you, Malevola, and mean to have it met.
Your wicked plans you'll find you'll quickly alter,
(*Aside*) She little thought the moon was in this quarter!
The Fairies of the Moon, by our direction,
This Princess shall take under their protection.
The child shall live, whate'er her trials may be,
And in the end this witch must yield to me.

Malevola   This is the strangest sight I e'er have seen,
The Man in the Moon's a Fairy Queen!
Who's she that thinks Malevola will bend,
Nor fight it with her to the bitter end?

Luna   Come, Fairy Moonbeams! — aid me with thy might,
'Tis Luna calls thee from the realms of night.

Malevola   Your chaff reserve for mortals — for myself,
I scorn the banter of a fairy elf!
To this king's banquet I intend to go,
Where you my strength and sovereignty shall know.

Luna   I've more resources than to her I'll own!

Malevola   (*aside*) My spells I'll cast tonight!

Act I, Scene 2

Malevola ⎱ (*together*) So now begone!
Luna ⎰

Malevola and Luna disappear

Thunder and lightning

Scene 2

The Royal Palace

General Dogsbody, Frivolette and the palace servants sing

Song 1

1st Maid (*speaking*) Well, Dogsbody, old thing, how goes it? Had a busy day? (*She kisses him on the cheek*)
Dogsbody Not so familiar, if you please.
2nd Maid Why, you're only the head butler.
Dogsbody I may be head butler, but please bear in mind ...

Frivolette comes forward. She carries his selection of hats on a tray

... that among the more or less important positions that I also occupy are those of Prime Minister (*he dons a bowler hat*), Commander in Chief (*general's helmet*), Chancellor of the Exchequer (*top hat*), and First Lord of the Admiralty (*admiral's cocked hat*) — so kindly treat me with the reverence and respect due to one of my exalted ranks.

The Maids curtsy

That's better! (*He gives Frivolette back the admiral's hat*) However, in my capacity of head butler you may all come round and buzz me if you like!

The girls crowd round and kiss him. There is a fanfare, off

The girls exit excitedly

Ah, Frivolette, what a day! What a day! What a successful function. I congratulate myself that in my capacity of Lord Chamberlain (*he dons a wig*) I have fairly excelled myself. Nothing omitted. Nothing forgotten. Oh, I'm a perfect marvel!

A Lackey enters

Lackey Make way for her Imperial Highness, the Princess Beauty!

Music: royal march

The Nurse enters carrying the baby Princess Beauty who wears a magnificent robe embroidered with the royal arms in gold. She is followed by a Maid carrying the crib; a Maid carrying a feeding bottle; a Maid carrying a powder puff; a Maid carrying a nappy; a Maid carrying a gold stool and the Nurse's bag

The stool is placed for the Nurse to sit on. She misses it, and sits on the floor. The baby flies up in the air. Dogsbody catches it

The Lackey and Maids bow/curtsy and exit

Dogsbody How fares our beloved Princess after the fatigue of the ceremony? May I dangle her?
Nurse (*taking the baby back*) Certainly not! I'm the only dangler on these premises. (*She puts the baby in the crib and tucks her in*)
Dogsbody I trust the nation's treasure is not tired?
Nurse Tired! That muddling Archbishop nearly drowned the little precious. Reminded me of the christening of my sister's boy — Bill Blastit!
Dogsbody Bill Blastit! How did your sister's boy get a name like Bill Blastit?
Nurse The vicar caught his knee on the font!
Dogsbody I see!

Dogsbody bows and exits, followed by Frivolette

The Baby howls

Nurse What is it, precious? Of course, of course, it's time for her bottle.

Act I, Scene 2

(*She takes the baby's bottle from her medical bag and gives it to Beauty*) Did naughty ol' Nan-nans forget Beauty's ickle-wickle bockle? Here, love, cop hold of that. Just look at the way she grabs it — just like her old man! She's having one quick. Which reminds me, it's time for mine an' all. (*She takes a Guinness bottle from her bag — a rubber one with a squeaker in the neck. To the audience*) Purely medicinal! Purely medicinal! It's the perfect cure for which there is no known disease! (*She takes a swig at the bottle, then squeezes it — squeak — under each armpit. She sings*)

Song 2

After the second verse a Victorian-style Stage Manager enters with an easel and a placard on which are printed the words of the chorus

The Nurse and the audience sing the chorus. At the end of the song the Nurse finishes her snort

(*Speaking*) Ah! That's better! Now where did I put my diddy-bag? Where is it? Ah, there we are. (*She picks up her bag and puts the Guinness into it*) I've just been doing me Christmas shopping. Isn't it awful? The tram was so crowded even the men were standing! Are you all enjoying yourselves? Are you? Why, what are you doing? Never mind. (*For a full house*) Good to see such a dense crowd here tonight. [(*For a poor house*) Good to see such an alert, intelligent, and select audience in tonight. Mind you, we have had smaller houses. Oh, yes. Last week the audience was so small we all got a cab and went to see a show. It was like Aberdeen on a flag day!] But I'm so happy to be back in (*local town*) once again. I am! I've got excellent digs in (*local posh area*). Oh, yes, I like to stay where the big knobs hang out. I said to my landlady, "It's very nice round here, but you must have trouble with the rates." She said, "Oh, we don't have rates — only maice!" Yes, I'm very fond of (*local town*). Years ago I used to have a boyfriend here. A gorgeous hunk of a man he was. I was wild about him. I adored him to distraction. I'd have followed that man to the ends of the earth! Well, I would have done, but he moved to Woking. I did go over there once, actually — but it was closed. (*She returns to her bag*) Look, that's got me christening present for the princess in it too. (*Showing the parcel*) But I'll tell you something — I don't trust some of the folk around here. Some of them have got very taking ways. Know what I mean? I know what! — Would you keep an eye on me bag for me? Would you? Look, I'll put it down there. Now, if anyone tries to nick me bag, will you all shout out "NANNY!" Will you? Then they'll know they've got me to deal with. Come on now, let's have a practice. I'll pretend to be pinchin' me bag, and you all yell out: "NANNY!" And I mean everyone. You too, sir! You don't mind me calling you sir, do you, sir? It's just in fun! Some women get older — I just get bolder. Here we go then. (*She approaches the bag. The audience shouts*) Have you started? (*Etc., etc., until a suitable volume is reached*) That's fine! Now at least I know that Beauty's little present will be safe. Ah, the bonny little ——

The Lackey enters, spots the bag, and makes for it

The audience shout. The Nurse chases the Lackey round the stage as far as the door. Loud fanfare. They stop in their tracks

Lackey (*announcing*) Their Royal Majesties, the King and Queen!

Music: regal march

The King and Queen enter, followed by Dogsbody, Frivolette, Lackeys, Maids, etc. They proceed to their thrones. The King carries a sceptre which he swings jauntily

King Well, Nurse, how fares our priceless little treasure?
Nurse Oh, most divinely, your majesty. Here she is, the precious, here she is! Ups-a-daisy!

The Nurse takes the baby out of the crib and tosses her up in the air and catches her. The King and Queen scream. The Queen faints and is caught by Dogsbody. Frivolette puts the stethoscope round Dogsbody's neck and the doctor's top hat on his head. He attends the Queen

King I've told you not to do that!
Queen Oh, my liver! My imperial liver!
Nurse Am I the Nurse or am I not?
King Oh, certainly, certainly, we wouldn't interfere for the world! Has the darling had her dinner?
Nurse Of course she has! (*Tossing baby up and down*) She's had her porridge, and her fish and chips, and her Newcastle Brown! and ——

Act I, Scene 2

Queen (*swooning*) Oh my love my love, her liver, her imperial liver!
Nurse Am I the Nurse, or am I ——
King Oh certainly, certainly, er, let me hold the precious, give her to me! Give her to me!
Nurse Mind you don't drop her, she's very brittle. I must go and see to her bottle ...

The Nurse trips and the baby flies through the air. The King catches her and passes her to the Queen, who faints again into Dogsbody's arms

Queen For heaven's sake get rid of that old hag!
King Certainly, dear. Get rid of the old hag.
Dogsbody Certainly, sire. Get rid of the bag!
Lackey Certainly, sir!

The Lackey picks up the Nurse's bag. The audience shouts. The Lackey drops the bag

   The Nurse chases the Lackey off

King Well, now that's settled we wish to make an announcement. Welcome all to our daughter's christening. Princess Beauty! There she is!
Dogsbody (*kneeling*) Princess Beauty!
All (*kneeling*) Princess Beauty!

   The Lackey returns

Lackey   My liege, the fairies now are ready at the door.
King   Admit them, we are ready. Say no more.
              Strike up a flourish of trumpets as they come,
              Likewise the cornet and the kettledrum!

Flourish without. Music

Fairies enter carrying gifts: Luna, a casket; Vedonia (beauty), a rose; Elegantia (grace), a chain of precious stones; Melodia (song), fairy bells; Camilla (dance), golden ballet shoes; Thalia (happiness), a golden chalice; Pamela (art), a laurel wreath

Luna   From my far celestial throne to Earth
             I come to bless this Royal Infant's birth.
             (*She presents the casket*)
             Within this crystal casket is enclosed
             A wondrous gem of purest dew composed,
             Conferring gifts beyond all human price,
             That Earth may be for her a Paradise.
             Inestimable treasure I impart —
             Sweet purity and kindliness of heart.

The Court applauds politely. Vedonia comes forward and presents the rose

Vedonia This rose bestows all outward loveliness,
             Beauty of form and wealth of gleaming tress,
             And eyes to hold all hearts beneath control —
             Sweet limpid mirrors of a lovely soul.

The Court applauds. Elegantia comes forward

Elegantia This chain of gems, which round thy neck I place,
              Shall add to Beauty, Daintiness and Grace,
              The subtle air of tenderness and charm —
              A woman's surest shield and strongest arm.

The Court applauds. Pamela presents the laurel wreath

Pamela   A radiant Princess, she shall play her part
             In all that is most beautiful in Art.

The Court applauds. Melodia presents silver bells

Melodia These bells denote the glorious gift of song,
             The notes of Philomel to thee belong;
             Through me each feathered songster of the glade
             With its sweet music now endows this maid.

Applause. Camilla presents the shoes

Camilla Thy step as light as gossamer shall be,
             And every movement graceful, bold, and free;

Act I, Scene 2   9

> Her dancing shall astonish every nation,
> She'll be the Génée of her generation.

Applause. Thalia comes forward with the chalice

Thalia   Sweet sunny temper, cheerfulness and mirth,
             Joyous contentment be thy lot on Earth.
Dogsbody (*with a town-crier's hat and bell*)
             Oh yes! Oh yes!! Know all men by these presents
             This babe has now been made perfection's essence!
Luna   Our many fairy duties call us hence,
             But look to us for your sweet babe's defence.

Thunder and lightning. The Lights fade up and down. The ladies scream. The Queen faints. General consternation

King Hello! What's up?
Dogsbody (*in a policeman's helmet*) As Chief of Police I have my suspicions!

A Lackey runs in

Dogsbody What is it?
Lackey   A party named Malevola's below!
King (*panicking*)   Malevola the Spiteful? Here's a go!
              Dogsbody! Queen! — for her there's no place ready!
Queen   Ho! Hi! I swoon! (*She faints*)
Dogsbody   She's fainted! Oh, dear lady!
              Is there no hartshorn or burnt feathers handy?
King   I think I'll try her with a nip of brandy!

Malevola enters

Malevola A pretty feast indeed! Now, tell me, pray,
              Why was I not invited here today?
              Why leave me out? You must have had some reason!
King   We meant to ask you — for the hunting season!
Malevola You bade all Fairyland, but I was flouted;
              It's very evident my power was doubted.
              So be it then! The gift that I've to give

	This baby princess is: "She shall not live!"
All gasp	
	Her sixteenth birthday — on that very day
	To spin a web of silk she will essay,
	And, as the wheel around and round shall fly,
	'Twill prick her finger, and she'll surely die!
Queen (*swooning*)	Collect and burn all spindles out of hand!
	Destroy each spinning wheel throughout the land!
King (*placing the admiral's hat on Dogsbody's head*)	
	As Lord High Skipper look alive and skip,
	Capstan and Compass take from every ship!
Queen	The Government of Egypt we shall wheedle
	To come and take away Cleopatra's needle!
Dogsbody (*in a town-crier's hat*)	
	Oh yes! Oh yes! Oh yes! and then, oh know —
	Our trumpeters this proclamation blow
	To save the Princess from this witch's power
	She is to be shut up within the Tower;
	And to make sure no spindle wounds her hand,
	Till she's sixteen, they're banished from the land!
	Each, now this proclamation has been read,
	Who dares a spindle keep, shall lose his head!
All	Well said!
Malevola	Kick at the spindle pricks! I have revealed
	You kick in vain, your infant's fate is sealed.
	As for my insult, here are gifts for you,
	Your amiable Queen will turn a shrew;
	You'll thus appreciate my bitter curse,
	Downhill you'll rush with speed from bad to worse.
	A luckless monarch, dogged by dire disaster,
	No-one shall run the road to ruin faster.
	The dragging up of your begifted brat
	Shall be in *poverty*! — I'll see to that.
	Your party system is all wrong, you see —
	When next you give one you'll remember me!
	Ah-ha-ha-ha!
Luna	But I have power still!
	The Princess I can surely save, and will!
	Should evil fates to your instructions keep,
	She shall not die, but only go to sleep!

Act I, Scene 2   11

General reaction

	When in her hand the spindle's wound is made
	For years I'll have the fatal end delayed.
	One hundred years shall pass in calm repose
	Lost to her friends, but guarded from her foes,
	Till there shall come a man of courage brave,
	Who, if he will, the Princess then may save.
	If he will fight to gain his darling's side,
	One kiss shall wake her — and she'll be his bride.
Malevola	Now pull the other leg! That's all my eye!
	The moment of my triumph has drawn nigh!
	You'll never find a prince all that to do!
	Romance and chivalry belong to few.
Luna	A prince shall rise of valour and renown,
	A prince well worthy of a famous crown,
	Who'll fight and conquer; so be well advised;
	You'll lose at last!
Malevola	I wouldn't be surprised!
	These Pantomime contentions — do *I* win 'em? Never!
Luna	Of course not. In (*town name*) virtue triumphs ever!
	Fairies begone!
Malevola	At any rate, I shall have done my duty!
Luna	And I'll do mine, for Britain, Home and Beauty!

Luna exits with the other Fairies

Malevola   Baaah! It isn't fair!

The frontcloth from Scene 1 descends behind Malevola, cutting off the King, Queen and the Court

Song 3

Malevola sings

Malevola exits at the end of the song

Scene 3

The Abode of Time

A backcloth of whirling planets and stars. There is a large hour-glass (trick prop). Set R is a big clock with a movable hand, with the scroll "TEMPUS FUGIT". The face of the dial marks years one to a hundred

Old Father Time enters polishing a scythe. The sound of hundreds of ticking clocks fade in, then there is a loud peal of electric bells off stage

Luna and the Fairies enter

Time	Who dares assail my fast and secret portals?
Luna	Is Father Time at home?
Time	No, not to mortals. Time's fixed routine on no condition varies.
Luna	But please ... we're Fairies!
Time	Ah! — Fairies! Then make your pretty selves at home with me. Doubtless, my dears, you'd like a cup of tea.

The top of the hour-glass falls over (trick prop) forming a dainty tea-table, with cups, saucers, cakes etc., fixed to it

Luna	Old Time! On Earth an infant has been born, Cherubic, cheerful, lovely as the morn, Will you — we'd feel so happy if you could — Bring her at once to dawning womanhood?
Time	I can't advance the clock for sprite nor man.
Luna	Surely to please a fairy, sir, you can?
Time	No, it can't be done.
Luna	Not even to please me?
Time	I tell you it can't be done!

Vedonia Disagreeable old pig!
Elegantia Grumpy old thing!
Pamela Cantankerous old fossil!
Melodia Opinionated old monster!
Camilla Surly old vagabond!
Thalia Ill-mannered old horror!
All And that's what we think of you!

Act I, Scene 4

Vedonia Come along, girls, we don't want any of his stodgy old teacakes!
Luna Now do be nice. If not, they'll all start crying!
Elegantia The cross old thing!
Time Now this is really trying!
Melodia We hate you! Don't we?
Fairies (*weeping*) Yes!
Time (*covering his ears*) No more of this!
Come here, my dears. Give Father Time a kiss.
Fairies We will if you'll consent.
Time I can't say no.

The Fairies all kiss Father Time. He crosses to the dial and puts the hand on sixteen years

It's done. You kissed me sixteen years ago!

There are hundreds of different clock chimes and bells! The Lights whirl furiously giving the illusion of planets spinning across the sky at high speed

Father Time exits, surrounded by Fairies who make a big fuss of him

Luna (*to the audience*)
Ah sisters, you can't all be fairies, we know,
But you must not feel out in the cold;
Remember, Old Time still allows you to grow
Very sweetly and gracefully old.
You will keep all your tender and womanly charm —
It's a gift that will not disappear —
When you feel Father Time lay his hand on your arm,
If you kiss him and call him a "dear"!

Luna exits

Scene 4

The Royal Palace

As Scene 2. It is sixteen years later and the Court is now bankrupt. There are signs everywhere of decay: furniture worn, people's clothes in tatters, everyone down at heel

The King is at the washtub. The Queen (now a scold) is ironing. Frivolette is hanging washing on a line. Dogsbody is scrubbing the floor. Maid and Lackeys are sweeping and cleaning

> **Song 4: Work, Boys, Work**
> **(To the air of "Tramp! Tramp! Tramp!" by F. Root as follows)**

Maids } (*ad lib*) Work, work, work, work, work, work, work, work,
Lackeys (*etc., etc.*)

The King comes forward, and finds a half-crown on the floor

King Here's a go! I've just found half a crown on the floor!
Queen (*coming forward, tapping the King on the shoulder*) Just a minute! Just a minute! What about the *two* half-crowns you owe me?
King Oh, er, yes, my dear. So I do. Here's one half-crown on account.

Dogsbody rises and comes forward

Dogsbody (*to the Queen*) Er, excuse me, your majesty, but may I remind you that you borrowed two half-crowns from the Exchequer. And I'm afraid I'm a little short.
Queen I know. It must be hell down there! Here you are then. One half-crown on account.
King Hang on, Dogsbody! Didn't you borrow two half-crowns from me?
Dogsbody For the Exchequer, your majesty, for the Exchequer! Quite so. Here's one half-crown on account.
King (*to the Queen*) I still owe you half a crown, don't I, my dear? Well, here it is. Now we're all fair and square.
Queen So I should think. Here, Dogsbody — for the Exchequer. Now we're all fair and square. (*She returns to her ironing*)
Dogsbody Thank you, your majesty. (*To the King*) And here's the other half-crown I owe your majesty. Now we're all fair and square. (*He returns to the scrubbing*)
King Thanks, Dogsbody. So, I found one half-crown, paid a two half-crown debt, and I've still got half a crown left over. Now that's what I call high financing! (*He sings*)

> I am not a wealthy man,
> But I've hit upon a plan

Act I, Scene 4

>That will render me as happy as a king!
>And if you will allow
>Me, I'll tell it to you now,
>For time, you know, is always on the wing.
>
>Work, boys, work, and be contented,
>As long as you've enough to buy a meal,
>For a man you may rely
>Will be wealthy by and by,
>If he'll only put his shoulder to the wheel.

All
>Work, boys, work, and be contented,
>As long as you've enough to buy a meal,
>For a man you may rely
>Will be wealthy by and by,
>If he'll only put his shoulder to the wheel.

Queen What's Dogsbody doing down there?
King He said he wanted a position in the penal service, my love.
Queen Well, what's he doing down there?
King I made him Governor of the Scrubs!
Dogsbody Things have gone from bad to worse, your majesty, and no mistake. That terrible Wicked Fairy has kept her word, and the country's broke! It's the recession, your majesty.
Queen Recession?
All Yes. (*To the audience*) Stop living beyond our means, you lot!
King It's no use worrying. I don't worry. I keep old Dogsbody here to do all the worrying for me — and pay him five pounds a week for it.
Queen But you're broke to the wide.
King Yes, my love, broke, that's it, broke!
Queen Well, how do you pay Dogsbody five pounds a week?
King I don't. That's one of the things he has to worry about! (*He sings*)
>Discontented people say
>All work and little play
>Will make a boy a blockhead as a rule,
>You can answer them and say
>"Never work and always play
>Will make him both a blockhead and a fool!"

All
>Work, boys, work, and be contented,
>As long as you've enough to buy a meal,

>   For a man you may rely
>   Will be wealthy by and by,
>   If he'll only put his shoulder to the wheel.

Queen I'm sorry I ever married you!
King Oh, my queen! You took me for better or worse.
Queen Yes, and you're a precious sight worse than I ever took you for! We've got the wolf at the door.
King I don't mind the wolf being at the door, but it's just had pups in the lobby. (*To Dogsbody*) You know, for twenty years my wife and I were ecstatically happy.
Dogsbody Then what happened?
King We met!
Queen What are you muttering about there?
Dogsbody Your majesty, the servants are all complaining. They say they've had stale bread every day this week.
Queen That's your responsibility. You're the Master of the Rolls! (*She sings*)

>   "You'll enjoy a quiet crust
>   More by rubbing off the rust"
>   It's a maxim that should never be forgot.
>   Honest labour leads to wealth,
>   And will give you inward health,
>   So it's best to be contented with your lot.

All
>   Work, boys, work, and be contented,
>   As long as you've enough to buy a meal,
>   For a man you may rely
>   Will be wealthy by and by,
>   If he'll only put his shoulder to the wheel.
>   (*Ad lib*) Work, work, work, work, work, work, work, work,
>   (*Etc., etc.*)

Frivolette, the Maids and Lackeys exit, taking the cleaning props and clothes line, etc.

King Where's Princess Beauty?
Dogsbody Ah, Princess Beauty! Sixteen this very day! I suppose she'll be thinking of getting married?

Act I, Scene 4   17

Queen   Married! No millionaire from Midas down to Coutts
              Is good enough to black my darling's boots!
King Well, as a matter of fact I've advertised in the *Exchange and Mart*
that eligible suitors can be received today. I'll go and see if any have
arrived!

The King and Dogsbody exit

Queen *(following)* Suitors! That's that scratch lot in the lobby, I suppose.
I took them for the rates and taxes!

She exits. Princess Beauty enters

Music: Song 5

Princess Daddy! Daddy! I thought I'd find my daddy here,
              I want to cheer him up, the poor old dear.
              Whilst all around are poverty and strife,
              I only see the beauteous side of life;
              And truthfully, take all the seasons round,
              A happier girl than I cannot be found.
              Yes, were I not a princess, I'd go wild
              Here, shut up ever since I was a child!

Nuts, the Princess's shaggy poodle dog, enters

Nuts!! Naughty boy! Where have you been? *(To the audience)* This is
Nuts, everybody. Say hello to the nice people, Nuts. That's right. *(To the
audience)* Come on, children, say "Hello, Nuts!" .... Oh, come on, you
can do better than that. Now altogether — "Hello, Nuts!" ... That's
better! *(Etc., etc.)* Would you like to see him do his tricks? ... Come on
then. Sit, Nuts!

Nuts sits

Beg, Nuts! Beg!

Nuts begs

Roll over, Nuts!

Nuts somersaults

   Die for your country, Nuts!

Nuts obeys

   A Street-Vendor, with bags on a tray, crosses the stage

Vendor Peanuts! Hot-roasted peanuts! Peanuts! Peanuts!

   The Street-Vendor exits

Nuts runs across to the proscenium arch and cocks up one leg

Princess Nuts! Don't you dare.

She chases Nuts away from the proscenium arch. He runs to the Nurse's bag, which he picks up in his mouth. The audience shouts

   The Nurse enters carrying the Princess's schoolbooks

She chases Nuts around the stage. He drops the basket back in its place

Nurse Ooooooh! That dog. You little horror. I'll skin you. Ah, Beauty, there you are. Come along now. It's time for your lesson.
Princess Nanny. Would you be angry with someone for something she didn't do?
Nurse For something she didn't do? No, of course not.
Princess Good.
Nurse Why?
Princess I didn't do my homework!
Nurse You cheeky young pretender! (*She sits and opens a book*) Your father's been asking for you. He's looking over your suitors.
Princess I know. I've seen them. I don't like the look of any of them.
Nurse Quite right, my love, you can't be too careful. My sister's husband has always been very slack in his appearance.
Princess Oh?
Nurse Yes, she hasn't seen him for fourteen years. And lazy! He was so lazy he only married her because she was a widow with five children.
Princess Oh Nanny, I don't want to marry any of those horrid sort of men. Oh, I wish I were free, Nanny, free as the wind.

Act I, Scene 4

Nurse Yes, I wish I was free of the wind.
Princess Nanny dear, I'll tell you a secret — a great big secret. I'm in love!
Nurse She's got it! Young girls take to love as easily as they do the measles.

The Lights begin to dim

Princess He's a prince. And, oh, so handsome. But not of this country. A strange, strange country, far away — I have often seen him in my dreams.

Through the gauze backing the Prince appears as if in the Princess's dream during the following

The Princess sings

Song 5

The Prince disappears at the end of the song

Nurse (*speaking*) Oh, it was all a dream. Well that's all right, then. You know what they say about dreams: Spit in your left hand, rub both hands together, and it'll all come true.
Princess Which is my left hand? I never can remember.
Nurse Oh, Beauty! How many more times? Mark, and inwardly digest.

Princess Beauty follows, marking the words with her own hands. Nuts follows her

>Now there's me right hand to begin with,
>And there's me left hand oppo-site.
>If I lose my left hand then my right hand is left,
>'Cos the only hand left is me right!
>So I must be left with me right hand,
>If I of my left am bereft;
>So it's logic'ly right,
>If I'm left with me right,
>I can write
>With me right,
>'Cos it's left!
>... Right?

Princess Right!
Nurse (*as she exits*) So then, go to it!

The Nurse exits

Music: Song 5. The Princess and Nuts spit into their left hand/paw and rub both hands/paws together

Princess Beauty smiles happily and exits, followed by Nuts

Malevola enters. She is palpably disguised in a slouch hat and a cloak of leaves and she carries a pedlar's tray

There is a hiss of cymbals and a green spot

Malevola Ah, ha! ha! ha! The sixteen years have passed,
And I shall get my dire revenge at last.
No-one will know me disguised as an old hag!
(*She produces the spindle*)
The spindle! (*She sees the Nurse's bag and crosses to it*)
Perhaps I'll hide it in this bag.

The audience shout

Perhaps I won't!

The Nurse enters

Nurse Good heavens! It's Mrs Pankhurst.
Malevola Come buy! Come buy! My novelties are cheap.
Nurse I can't afford to buy but only peep.
Malevola Pray look, fair dame, with these you must be tempted.
Nurse My purse, most sad to say, has long been emptied.
Malevola Say, where does yon mysterious portal lead?
Nurse Oh, to some secret chamber, I've been told.
Malevola It might contain a countless store of gold!
Nurse The key's been lost for sixteen years.
Malevola Dear me!
That's curious! I possess a magic key;
The key, I fancy, to the situation.

Act I, Scene 4

>It may bring joy to this distressful nation.
>Fair maid, 'tis yours! (*She gives the Nurse the key*)
>>I'll take the thanks I earn
>After my key has done you its good turn!

Nurse I've always wanted to know what was the other side of this door!

She opens the door and enters. The Lights come up behind the gauze, and we see a spinning-wheel which the Nurse approaches behind the gauze

Malevola   Time flies apace, and ev'ry grain of sand
>Now hastens on the vengeance I have planned;
>As stronger proves the Moon Fairy or I,
>So shall the princess sleep, or she shall die!

Nurse A spinning wheel! Merciful heavens! I must tell his majesty at once. (*Running out of the room*) Majesty! Sire! Someone!

The Nurse exits

The Lights fade behind the gauze

Malevola   The contest for supremacy begins,
>A stubborn fight 'twill be, whoever wins!
>Come all ye powers of darkness, take my part!
>And lend me the aid of magic art.
>I'm ready now, and eager for the fray;
>If I'm successful, Beauty dies today.

Malevola goes through the secret door and exits

Princess Beauty enters

Music: Introduction to the "spinning-wheel chorus" begins

Princess   I don't think everybody should have gone
>And left me on my birthday all alone;
>And what's the reason, pray, of all this fuss?
>As if some fearful danger threatened us.

Princess Beauty exits

Music: Spinning-wheel chorus "Gretchen Am Spinnrade" by Franz Schubert. The Lights darken

During the following, through a gauze, on the wall at the back of the stage, the Lights come up slowly on a vision of many witches at their spinning wheels. There is a golden spinning wheel in the centre

Witches (*singing*)   Magic spells we weave,
                  And fortunes win;
                  The wheel turns, the wheel turns the future
                  Which fate shall spin.

                  The murmuring wheels,
                  Through silken reels,
                  Shall soothe the mind
                  Of all mankind.
                  We live and spin,
                  But spin not to live,
                  True rapture we win
                  As rapture we give.

Princess Beauty enters

The Witches' singing continues (see page 23) over the following dialogue

Princess   What's that? What's that? 'Tis music I declare.
                  There's no-one here. It comes from ev'rywhere!
                  Why! Who are these girls I appear to see?
                  Say, are they there? Or only seem to be?
                  How beautiful the hum of all those wheels!
                  I'd simply love to spin those silken reels,
                  And sing that song in time.

Malevola enters

Malevola   So shall you do!

The wall at the back of the stage opens to reveal fully the Witches and the golden spinning-wheel

Act I, Scene 4

Princess   I never heard you come in. Who are you?
Malevola I am your patron, slave, and fairy friend.
All good things that you have, to you I send.
I watch you daily, keep you from all ill,
I've loved you ever, and will do so still.
Today's your birthday, and my present's here —

She leads the Princess up to the golden spinning-wheel

A golden spinning-wheel I've brought you, dear.
You'd like to learn?
Princess   Oh, yes! I wish I could.
Malevola You sit down there, dear!
Princess   Yes.
Malevola   I thought she would.
My dear, that tale they've told you 's all a swindle.
There! Look at that!

She fixes the spindle to the spinning-wheel

Princess   What is it?
Malevola   It's a spindle!
Ha! Ha! Take care! It's sharp and should it give
A wound, the suff'rer cannot longer *live*!
Witches (*singing during the above dialogue, i.e. from the Princess's entrance*)
Magic Spells we weave,
And fortune win;
The wheel turns, the wheel turns the future
Which fate shall spin.

The bobbins are flying,
Mysterious hum;
Now she who would try
Her skill, must come;
Obey the command
And lend us her hand
To turn fortune's wheel
That she may understand.
Offer her soul to
The Universe.

>   Her hand shall —
>   Escape not — the curse!

As the Witches sing the word "Curse!", and Malevola utters the word "live!", Malevola pushes the princess's hand on to the spindle

Princess   Oh, my! I've hurt my hand!
Malevola   A wound? Ha! Ha!
Princess (*staggering downstage, collapsing*)
                   Oh, help! I faint! I die! Mamma! Papa!

The Lights upstage fade, and the wall closes behind her

Malevola   Complete success so far attends me plan!
               Now, Fairy Queen, save Beauty if you can!

The Nurse runs on, followed by the King, Queen, Dogsbody, Frivolette Nuts and Servants, etc.

Nuts runs to the Princess and licks her hand in great distress

>   Hold there! You deemed I could outwitted be,
>   When many years ago you slighted me.
>   I told you then that I should make you smart
>   And ere this, tear your darling from your heart!
>   Revenge at last! You see, I've kept my word!

Luna enters

Luna   No! I am here. Your deep design I heard.
Malevola   Begone! She dies! And from this fated hour
               Show me the one who dare dispute my power!
Luna   Behold! I am here. And know with hearts more true,
               We Fairies keep our words as well as you.
  (*To the King and Queen*)
               Trust the princess to me, and calm your fears;
               She shall not die, but sleep — a hundred years.
Nurse   A hundred years! We'll all be dead by then,
               And all things changed before she walks again.
Dogsbody   Then, railways out of date, balloon-trains will

Act I, Scene 4

	Start from a station on the Hog's Back Hill.
King	No ships will then be sent to sea to sink.
Queen	Nobody take intoxicating drink.
Dogsbody	Then cent for cent on gas be realized.
Ladies	The female vote at last be recognized!
All	Too late!
Luna	Not so! These charmèd years shall fly,

Nor seem as many minutes passing by,
Though Malevola we cannot quite oppose,
She'll find 'gainst death we can exchange a doze.

The Princess's bed is revealed behind the gauze. The others gently place her on it

                    For we, the spirits of the stars, shall call
                    To meet her with her husband — one and all.
                    From yonder Moon we'll o'er her vigils keep,
                    Until a king's son's kiss shall wake her sleep.
Malevola   A lover's kiss? Ho! Ho! She'll sleep for ever!
                    From all the world this palace I will sever;
                    The princess with dense forests I'll surround;
                    No mortal foot shall reach her. Ha! ha!

Malevola exits with an evil laugh

A gauze of an exterior view of the palace, followed by two gauzes of "The Dense Forest" descend gently during the following

Luna   Around
                    Each one I cast my soothing spell;
                    On King, Queen, Courtiers, birds and beasts as well!
                    In morphous garden fair of sweetest sleep,
                    All here, unharmed, shall rest in slumber deep.

The King, Queen, Nurse, Dogsbody, Frivolette, Nuts, etc, fall asleep and gradually collapse. Finally, Luna is left alone in front of "The Dense Forest"

                    Sleep, Beauty, sleep, so sweet, so fair,
                    In trustful innocence surrender.

> The hand of Time shall gently spare
> A flower so exquisitely tender.
>
> Sleep while a hundred troubled years
> Roll on, with human anguish teeming,
> Safe from all turmoil, strife, and fears,
> May Love's own angels bless thy dreaming.
>
> Dream on, till one pure rapturous kiss
> Shall harbinger a wondrous morrow.
> Then awake! to all the radiant bliss
> Of Love triumphant over sorrow.

Luna exits

The humming "Spinning-wheel chorus" continues into and through the next scene

Witches (*singing*)
> Eternal sleep!
> Eternal sleep!
> Which naught may o'erthrow, but
> A true lover's kiss!
> Which naught may o'erthrow, but
> A lover's kiss!
> Hmmmmmmmmmmmmmmmmmmm, (*etc., etc.*)

Scene 5

The Abode of Time

The humming "spinning-wheel chorus" continues. There are clocks ticking as before. Church bells toll gently. The Lights are whirling as at the end of Scene 3. The hand on the large dial turns steadily from one towards a hundred during the scene

Father Time enters with his scythe, with which he makes rhythmical mowing movements as he crosses the stage

Act I, Scene 5

Time
    A hundred years go by,
    I hear the tramping feet;
    And some there pass that sigh,
    And some have memories sweet.
    A hundred years are sped,
    Through darkness comes the morn;
    In heaven overhead
    The star of hope is born!

A new star in cloth lights up brilliantly

    Do thou, sad bells, a hundred times
    Toll out the passing year;
    Do thou, glad bells, with joyous chimes,
    Peal forth the new-born clear.
    A hundred times,
    A hundred chimes,
    Loud, clear, and long.
    Ding-dong! Ding-dong!

Distant church bells are heard

    Pass on, oh! hundred springs!
    Thou hundred summers, go!
    For Love hath lent ye wings,
    The fairest earth shall know.

He raises his scythe in salutation

    A hundred autumns' tears,
    A hundred Christmas' chime
    I greet, who made these years.
Chorus of voices (*off*)
    All hail! Old Father Time!

The Lights fade to Black-out just before the hands on the dial reach 100

Scene 6

The Dense Forest

As at the end of Scene 4

Obadiah I and Obadiah II have been trying to cut down a large tree (perhaps painted on a backcloth) without success. Obadiah I is a young, dopey yokel with a straw stuck permanently in his mouth. Obadiah II is very old, with a long white beard

Obadiah I   Upon this wood, to use a strong expression,
I'm blowed if I can make the least impression.
(*He raises his hat to a lady in the audience*)
I've cut down nothing, though I've cut all day,
And now the evening's come, I'll cut away.

He raises his hat again to the lady in the audience, then throws his axe to the ground. Obadiah II strikes him on the head with his axe handle — sound effect

That was my 'ead you 'eard!
Obadiah II   Then it's an 'ard 'un.
It's spoilt moi axe, so you must ask moi pardon!

He giggles. Obadiah I raises his hat to the lady in the audience

'Ere! Why do you keep raisin' yer 'at to that lady? Do you know 'er?
Obadiah I   (*raising his hat*) No, but me brother does.
Obadiah II   Then why do you keep raisin' yer 'at to er?
Obadiah I   It's me brother's 'at!
Obadiah II   I don't wish to know that! 'Ere! —
Now look at that, you've finished all the beer!
Obadiah I   Well, let's drink something else.
Obadiah II   No ruddy fear!
Obadiah I   'Ow about summat to eat?
Obadiah II   Eat! Eat! Don't you ever think about anything but eating?
Obadiah I   Yes. Sometimes I think about girls.
Obadiah II   When do you think about girls?
Obadiah I   When I'm eating! Let's have a pomegranate!
Obadiah II   (*nodding his head towards the bag*) Ahrr! Some o' *them*!

Act I, Scene 6

Obadiah I Some o' these?
Obadiah II (*nodding his head at other bags*) No, *them*!
Obadiah I (*picking up the second bag*) These 'ere?
Obadiah II No, them there!
Obadiah I (*picking up the first bag*) Ain't these them?
Obadiah II (*nodding at the third bag*) No. Them's them. Where I'm noddin'!
Obadiah I Oh, these is them?
Obadiah II Ay, that's right. Them's they! Give 'em 'ere! (*He snatches up the bag and pours out the pomegranates. There are ten*)
Obadiah I 'Ere! Fair do's! Fair do's! These is those I wanted. Fair do's!
Obadiah II Roit! One for you. (*He gives one to Obadiah I*) One for me. Two for you. (*He gives Obadiah I another one*) One, two for me! (*He takes another two for himself*) Three for you. (*Another one for Obadiah I*) One, two, three for me. (*He takes three for himself. This leaves one, which he gives to Obadiah I*) Four for you. (*He takes back all four of Obadiah I's*) One, two, three, four for me!

Obadiah II has ten, Obadiah I has none

Roit?
Obadiah I Roit!

Obadiah II scoops the pomegranates back into the bag. There is a rumbling sound and a distant hiss of escaping air from above

Prince's voice (*from above*) Ahoy! Ahoy!
Obadiah I Aha! What sounds be these?
Prince's voice (*from above*) Ahoy! Ahoy!
Obadiah II It is the goblins of this demon wood!
    Oh take me somewhere!
Obadiah I   Oh, how I wish I could!
Prince's voice (*from above*) Ahoy! Ahoy!
Obadiah I (*shouting upwards*)
    Oh, say what you'd like done.
    We are two orphans — father and his son.
Obadiah II (*shouting upwards*)
    Yes, he's an orphan, and I am another —
    We don't possess no father nor no mother!
Prince's voice (*from above*) Ahoy! Ahoy!

There is now a violent hiss of air from above. Music: descending arpeggios. The two Obadiahs hide, terrified, behind trees

A balloon basket containing the Prince (wearing goggles) descends, followed by the deflating balloon itself. (This could be a cut-out, all wired from above)

Prince (*removing his goggles*) Well, we made it — and in one piece. (*He slaps his thigh*) But it is a bit of a nasty fix to be sure. Still, we've been in worse! (*He taps the balloon affectionately*) Soon get old "Nelly" repaired and aloft again. She's been with us ever since I can remember. Why, she's like one of the family. (*He sings*)

Song 6

The Stage Manager enters with the words for the audience

Everyone joins in the chorus. At the end of the song, both Obadiahs creep out nervously

Prince Hello there! Who might you two be?
Obadiah I Obadiah, an't please yer, mister.
Obadiah II (*wheezing nervously*) Same y'ere.
Prince He doesn't sound too well.
Obadiah I Oh, 'e gets winded playing draughts.
Obadiah II You can talk. 'E wants to be a sex maniac, but 'e keeps failing the medical!
Prince That's sad.
Obadiah II Ahr! But 'e does bird impressions.
Prince Bird impressions?
Obadiah II Ahr, 'e eats worms!
Prince Do not be concerned with us, my dear good men,
Direct us to some city if you can.
Obadiah II City? Rash youth! The wood is endless quite.
Go on and on and on, 'tis always night.
'Tis full o' creepin' things and goblin trees.
Prince I *seek* adventures, old man, such as these.
Has no-one ever lived here but yourselves?
Obadiah II Not in my time, except the forest elves.
When I was young — I'm ninety-five, yer know —
I heard some stories of the long ago ——

Act I, Scene 6   31

Prince Ninety-five! He's very lively for *ninety-five!*
Obadiah I Oh ahr. 'E remembers 'e's supposed to chase girls, only 'e keeps forgettin' why!
Prince   You interest me much, old man, proceed.
Obadiah I   'E's gettin' at you, sir, 'e is indeed!
Obadiah II   A princess ... in a palace ...
Obadiah I   In the air!
Obadiah II   She has to sleep, our woodman-tales declare,
                 Until some day she's wakened ... by a lover ...
Prince   Then I at once this princess shall discover!
Obadiah I   Suppose she's gotta lover!
Obadiah II   'Twould be queer!
                 She's been asleep for nigh one hundred year!
                 A watch the Fairies from the moon do keep
                 Upon the princess and her court asleep
                 Until a king's son kissing her shall break
                 The magic spell, when everyone shall wake.
Prince   Kiss the princess! Consider it done!
                 I am the man. (*He slaps his thigh*)
Obadiah I }
Obadiah II } (*together*) Are you, then, a king's son?
Prince   Ay! Every inch!

Both Obadiahs kneel

                          I'll fix up the balloon.
                 And take a quick excursion via the moon!
                 You'll lend a hand?
Obadiah II   Not me! I'm off.

Obadiah II exits

Obadiah I   I'll stay.
              I'd like to see this palace right away.
Prince   Good man! If only I could have the chance
              To be an ancient hero of romance!
              To rescue beauteous damsels in distress;
              To save from death this charming young princess.
              To overcome magicians in fair fight.
              Put ogres, giants, wizards, all to flight.

>   Alas! The days of chivalry are fled,
>   And wizards, witches, fairies all are dead.
>   While, as for me — I have been born too late —
>   For all the world is dull and up to date.

Luna appears

The Prince is startled. Obadiah I is terrified

Luna   Pray don't disturb yourself but list to me,
              The Fairy Luna, who has come to be
              Your guide to the enchanted station where
              You'll find my car to take you through the air.
              There!

Luna points with her wand to the first gauze behind which there now appears a fantastical Jules Verne-type flying machine

              Pass at once and turn into the thicket.
Obadiah I Ask her if she issues a return ticket!

The gauze rises and the Prince approaches the flying machine

Luna   My lunar power shall aid in your recovery
              After your voyage.
Prince   Startling discovery!
              I'll win this maid. To rescue her I'll fly.
              Goblins and poisons, bah! I can but die.
              To valiant knights the most congenial duty
              Is that which bids them rescue helpless beauty.

The Prince and Obadiah I enter the machine

Luna   Our fairy plots shall be concluded soon.
              Come, Fairy Sprites, and fly them o'er the moon.
              Down on the enchanted palace to descend,
              Happily, as decreed, our tale to end.

Hissing and music as before — in reverse direction. The flying machine

Act I, Scene 6

rises about six feet from the ground. The gauze sinks to the floor, simulating the machine's ascent. Misty clouds cover the stage (dry ice)

A vertical diorama is revealed upstage representing a bird's eye view of the landscape beyond the forest. It slowly rolls downwards to simulate the flying machine's ascent into the heavens: the horizon, a rainbow, sunbeams, wind, clouds, stars and planets, all represented by their traditional astrological symbols which appear in turn on the diorama and descend

> Planets and stars I now require your aid
> Until this prince his voyage safe hath made.
> Watch o'er his aerial ship as she floats higher,
> And make it safe as Plimsoll might desire.
> To aid his flight above this world of strife
> I'll lend the Rainbow! — sign of peaceful life;
> And in his favour shall my power put forth
> To quell the stormy spirit of the North!
> I'll fetch the Sunbeam that retires, and then
> Rises and shines o'er all the world again;
> While Zephyr, spirit of the Western Gales
> Shall waft him incense from her flowery vales.
> *(She waves her wand)*
> 'Tis well! Be scattered clouds, and let us gaze
> On him whose chivalry demands our praise!

Voices, off, sing the chorus to Song No. 6

CURTAIN

ACT II

Scene 1

The Abode of Time

As Act I Scene 3

When the CURTAIN *rises, Father Time is discovered with an armful of flowers and plants, etc., which he hands to Luna as he speaks*

Music background

Time	While Beauty's slept the days have swiftly flown,
	And each one has an interest of its own.
	The Spring brings forth the tender Valentine,
	And then the yellow Primrose is the sign
	That Eastertide draws near, to pave the way
	For blossoms sweet to crown the Queen of May.
	The Summer brings her Roses white and red,
	When rosy petals bloom and none are shed.
	When in the meadows mid the new-mown Hay
	Are men at work, while happy children play
	Till Autumn when the Harvest's safe in store,
	And sportsmen in the stubble range once more,
	While Leaves are falling, falling thick and fast
	To show the year will soon be of the Past.
	To Beauty, in her dreams, thus may we show
	How, year by year, the swift days come and go.
Luna	Though she must sleep till mortal penetrates
	To where she lies and rescue still awaits,
	Her saviour is at hand, remember this,
	Fair Beauty shall awake with Love's first kiss.

Malevola enters

Act II, Scene 2

Malevola You're mistaken, lady! I've taken care
Of that. Though now he travels through the air,
O'er seas and deserts, plains of burning sand, —
The tangled forests of this cursèd land,
Still by daybreak a thousand miles will part
Him from the petted darling of your heart.
And never fret — she'll sleep more safely here
Than if she rested in his palace fair.
My Fiery Dragon is both big and strong ...

Fearful roar without

She will be quite secure, however long
She sleeps. A Dragon makes a fine stronghold,
And guards her well from all of mortal mould.

Roar again

So fly your gallant prince here if you will,
And see if he can help you with his skill.
Why both your strengths combined will not suffice
To rouse that maiden, or unclose her eyes.
Sealed by my art, they cannot opened be
Until she has fulfilled her destiny.
Beauty will wake again, but not till you
Shall long have been forgotten — so adieu!

A flash

Father Time, Luna and Malevola disappear

SCENE 2

A Grand Corridor in the Royal Palace

A cloth with a deep perspective design. Painted on the cloth are lackeys and maids, etc., lying about asleep

Music: introduction to Song 7

Dogsbody enters in a nightshirt and nightcap sleepwalking

Song 7

The Royal Housemaids enter in their nighties, also sleepwalking, and giggling. They pursue Dogsbody, who exits, followed by the Housemaids

The music continues

The King enters in a nightgown and with a large sultan's turban. He is sleepwalking. There is a comedy dance. He sings

The Housemaids return again, but now wearing yashmaks like slave girls. They surround the King and make a fuss of him

The King continues singing

The Housemaids carry the King off. One picks up the Nurse's bag. The audience shouts. She drops the bag and flees. The Nurse enters in a nightdress but wearing a bridal veil and carrying a bouquet

Nurse   It's really most upsetting,
Why, asleep for years I've been;
There's not the slightest doubt of it
I'm always in a dream.
Old memories come flooding back,
It really is not fair,
Whilst they all have their gorgeous dreams,
I've had the same nightmare

She sings

Song 8

After two verses the Stage Manager, in a nightshirt, enters with the words. The King, Dogsbody and the Queen enter and join in the chorus

Wedding tableau. Then the Nurse, Dogsbody, King and Queen sing the chorus from Song 7

Act II, Scene 2A   37

Everyone exits at the end of the song

Music: "Beautiful Galathea" by Franz von Suppé (omit the opening flourish)

1. Cadenza-like passage for horn, woodwind, and flute

   Luna enters. As she speaks the scene-cloth is raised to reveal the forest gauzes, through which we see the sleeping princess in a pool of light

One by one the gauzes are raised

Luna So must it be. Within the forest's heart
Imprisoned there by Witch's deadly art,
Our princess too has dreamed as she has slept
One hundred years, while watch o'er her we've kept.
For though I've powerless been to break the spell
And waken her, she's still alive and well.
What are her thoughts? Come, magic power supreme,
Reveal to us — the Princess Beauty's dream!

Scene 2A

The Harlequinade: Princess Beauty's Dream

Music: "Beautiful Galathea" continues

2. Muted strings with bass pizzicato

Beauty (or Beauty's double wearing a mask) as Colombine sits up in her bed in a trance. Harlequin (Prince), masked, is revealed by a spotlight, standing beneath a moon. He holds out his arms to Beauty. She leaves the bed, and goes to him. They take hands, and dance a short *pas de deux*. As they come downstage of the bed, the Harlequinade-cloth descends slowly behind them cutting off the bed. They embrace, and on the very last note they kiss

3. Brief repeat of horn passage

Pantaloon enters downstage. From the opposite side Policeman enters upstage, and crosses the stage, saluting Pantaloon as he passes. Pantaloon waves on Butcher who is following downstage pushing his handcart. (This has a frame above it from which hang various joints of meat, poultry, rabbits, sausages, etc.) Meanwhile, six choirboys cross the stage briskly followed by Parson. The choirboys exit. Parson stops to say good-day to Policeman.

Pantaloon spies Harlequin embracing Colombine. Followed by Policeman (with his truncheon), Butcher (carrying a long knife-sharpener), and Parson, Pantaloon crosses to Harlequin and raises his stick to strike him. Harlequin turns and waves his magic bat at them

4. Cymbal crash!

All four are frozen like statues

5. Brisk Allegro

Following the crash, Harlequin runs off with Colombine. Nuts enters, runs over and briefly inspects the frozen four, sniffs at them, then spies the Nurse's handbag. He approaches it as if to pick it up. The audience shouts. Clown (Nurse) enters and chases Nuts off. Clown gives the thumbs-up sign to the audience, then notices the frozen four

6. Broad Counter Melody

Clown rearranges them:
a) Parson with rear leg up in air, pointing backwards behind him.
b) Butcher with his sharpener pointing at Policeman's bottom.
c) Policeman with his truncheon poised in the air above Pantaloon's head.
d) Clown hangs a string of sausages over Parson's raised foot by means of a loop at one end

7. Repeat of Brisk Allegro

Clown pulls the sausages tight, raising Parson's foot a few inches higher, then releases the sausages which causes:

Act II, Scene 2A   39

> Parson's foot to fly forward, and
> Kick Butcher's bottom, which makes
> Butcher's sharpener shoot forward, and
> Hit Policeman's bottom, which makes
> Policeman's truncheon come down on Pantaloon's head.

Pantaloon collapses on the floor. They all revive.

Policeman spies Clown shaking with laughter. He blows his whistle and chases after Clown, who exits running. Butcher spies the sausages around Parson's foot. Parson removes the sausages, dumps them in Butcher's hands in disgust, and exits in a huff. From the opposite side, Columbine runs in backwards waving farewell to Harlequin off stage

8. Orchestral Outburst

Pantaloon grabs Columbine by the hand and passes her so that she is between himself and Butcher. Butcher kneels, and presents her with the sausages. She shakes her head crossly. Pantaloon says yes! — take them! She grabs the sausages and dumps them into Pantaloon's hand. Meanwhile, Butcher has taken a large turkey from his cart which he presents to her. Pantaloon says take it! She takes the bird and gives it to Pantaloon. From his breast pocket Butcher (on his knees) takes out his heart (cardboard cut-out), and presents it to Colombine. Nuts has entered, and now runs between them, grabbing the heart which he puts in his mouth, and runs off downstage, pursued by Butcher.

Columbine stamps her foot in anger at Pantaloon. He offers her the turkey to placate her. It leaps into the air and flies off (on line). He holds out sausages towards her. Nuts enters upstage and runs between them, grabs the sausages, and runs off downstage in the opposite direction pursued by Pantaloon. Columbine exits. Butcher enters and returns to his cart

9. Short Flute Cadenza

As Butcher returns, Policeman enters from the opposite side and crosses the stage saluting Butcher as he passes. As he does so Nursemaid (Queen) enters with a baby in a large pram which she parks below the cart. Policeman salutes Nursemaid and exits. Butcher greets Nursemaid and admires the baby. They both cross to the upstage side of the cart to choose her meat.

Clown enters chasing a butterfly (which is attached to his head by a long, stiff wire), attempting to catch it with a butterfly net. He spies the baby in the pram. He hangs his butterfly apparatus on the cart, and peers into the pram.

10. Waltz

Clown takes the baby's bottle out of the pram and has a swig from it. The baby howls. He tells it to shush! It continues howling. He takes the baby out of the pram, pats it, shakes it, and finally hangs it on a meat hook on the cart frame. The baby stops howling. Clown takes down a large joint of meat which he wraps in the baby's shawl, and places in the pram in its stead. He creeps off, swigging the milk.

Followed by Butcher carrying her purchase, Nursemaid returns to her pram with another baby's bottle, which she goes to give to the baby, discovers the joint, sees the baby on the hook, snatches up the joint, hits Butcher over the head with it, and chases him round the cart. Policeman enters. Nursemaid runs to him and indicates what Butcher has done. Meanwhile, Butcher has returned the baby to the pram. Policeman crosses to Butcher followed by Nursemaid. Butcher indicates that the baby is back in the pram. They move around the cart in altercation, Butcher protesting his innocence.

Nuts, meanwhile, enters. He hangs the baby back on the hook and climbs into the pram. Nursemaid comes round the cart with the baby's bottle, followed by Policeman and Butcher still arguing. She sticks the bottle into Nuts' mouth, double-takes, and faints into the arms of Policeman

11. Brisk Allegro

Nuts jumps out of the pram and runs off with the baby's bottle. Policeman tosses Nursemaid into the arms of Butcher and runs off after Nuts, blowing his whistle. Nursemaid revives, slaps Butcher's face and exits with the pram after Policeman.

Harlequin runs on from one side. Columbine runs on from the other. They meet in the centre. Columbine gestures wildly, and indicates that Pantaloon plans to marry her (*indicating ring on finger*) to Butcher. As soon as Butcher sees them he runs to the entrance and calls on Pantaloon, who appears and chases Harlequin off with his stick. Harlequin blows Columbine a kiss, and runs off pursued by Pantaloon. Butcher kneels to Columbine, offering her a large black pudding (in a ring). She tosses her head and exits. During this, Parson enters upstage, followed by his six

Act II, Scene 2A   41

choirboys. The boys stop upstage of the cart — three either side of it — as the Parson continues and exits.

Nuts runs on and snatches the black pudding from Butcher, who still has it held out towards Columbine. He rises to chase Nuts, but now the Choirboys run off with the remaining six joints, birds, rabbits, sausages, etc., hanging on the cart frame, with Butcher starting to pursue each of them in turn.

As the last boy runs off Policeman enters. Butcher points after the boys. Policeman exits in pursuit.

Butcher stamps in fury, and pushes off his hand-cart upstage, which is now bare. Pantaloon enters downstage from the opposite direction, dragging on Columbine who wears a bridal veil over her face. Parson enters from the opposite downstage entrance, looking for the Choirboys. Pantaloon meets him centre, raises Columbine's bridal veil to reveal that she is Columbine, and indicates that he wants Parson to marry her to someone. He calls on Butcher, who returns

12. Final Waltz

Pantaloon joins Butcher's and Columbine's hands, and indicates that these are the pair he wants married. Parson nods agreement, bows to the three of them, and crosses to the other side of the stage where he comes face to face with Harlequin who enters with another bride wearing an identical veil to Columbine's. Harlequin raises her veil and reveals that it is Clown in disguise. Parson nods, bows, and crosses back to the other side of the stage, upstage, where he meets a third bride identically veiled. Pantaloon greets her and raises her veil to reveal it is the Nursemaid whom he, Pantaloon, wishes to marry! Parson nods, and crosses UC facing the audience. The three couples line up in front of him, backs to the audience. Nuts runs on with the black pudding in his mouth. Butcher sees him and chases after him as he runs off again through the downstage entrance

13. Final Gallop

The others have all turned round, and now
        Pantaloon chases after Butcher, downstage
        Nursemaid chases after Pantaloon,
        Parson chases after Nursemaid,
        Harlequin chases after Parson,

Columbine chases after Harlequin,
Clown chases after Columbine.

In the opposite direction Policeman chases the six Choirboys across the stage, upstage. As they exit upstage Nuts enters from the other side upstage leading the other chase across the back followed by Butcher, Pantaloon, Nursemaid, Parson, Harlequin, Columbine, and Clown. The Choirboys, pursued by Policeman, enter downstage in the opposite direction. They mark time two thirds of the way across, running on the spot. Nuts enters downstage and catches them up. The two chases join, running on the spot. Policeman looks over his shoulder, sees Nuts, blows his whistle, and they all about turn. Clown now leads the chase off downstage the way they have just come, and leads them on again upstage.

They run round in a circle c in general confusion, then break up so that they are left with Parson upstage facing the three couples once more. Parson gives the blessing, and the couples are married. They turn and face downstage. The brides lift their veils and the bridegrooms kiss their brides. But Harlequin has married Columbine, Butcher has married the Nursemaid, and Pantaloon has married the Clown! Everybody double-takes, then faints to the floor, except Harlequin and Columbine who stand triumphant over them all

Black-out

A single spotlight comes up on Malevola

Malevola   Fools! Fools! Fools!
To dream on happy bliss!
Why there's no crumb
Of hope he'll come
To wake her with his kiss!

The Lights come up for the following scene

Scene 3

Outside the Palace

Frontcloth as at the end of Act I, Scene 4

Act II, Scene 3   43

Malevola continues

Malevola   My bitter curse on all that dream
                To thwart the assembled hosts of ill!
                Forgiveness sweet to fools may seem,
                Revenge! — Revenge! — is sweeter still!
                Come, Dragon, from your poisoned lair,
                All loathly shapes that crawl and creep,
                Goblins and furies from the air,
                Vile, grizzly monsters from the deep!

Malevola exits. The Dragon enters

There is the sound of the Prince's airship approaching

Dragon   The forest echoes warn me from the air
                Some alien bird's descending on my lair.
                For such presumption he must dearly pay —
                Another victim will be mine today!
                And he who comes here now shall meet the fate
                Of all who try to pass my palace gate!
                Ahhhhhhhhhhhhhhhhr!

The Dragon retreats. The Prince's airship descends and the Prince emerges followed by Obadiah I

Prince   Yes, this must be the place — these dismal towers
                May well be the abode of evil powers.
Obadiah I   I heard strange sounds as o'er the wood we passed,
                Some queer old voices mingling with the blast,
                And Goblin spirits from the earth did rise
                Like they would fain have plucked us from the skies!

The Dragon roars off stage

                Oh Lor' — I'll go to our 'ouse! What was that?
Prince(*shielding Obadiah I*) Take cover, Obadiah, I smell a rat!

Malevola appears

There is a roll of drums throughout the following

Malevola	Madman! Thou darest pit thy puny skill
	Against the countless hosts who work my will?
Prince	He is thrice armed who draws the sword of right
	And truth against the hoards of lawless might.
	All fairyland will shield, inspire and aid
	The knight who faces peril unafraid.
Malevola	So be it, fool! I set my legions free.
	Thy folly shall destroy itself and thee!
	What ho, my minions, Satellite and Vassal,
	Guard well the portals of our silent castle;
	A daring Prince comes on to the attack,
	I charge you one and all to drive him back!

Malevola exits

Music. There is a great and wild combat scene to be worked here. The boughs of the trees (wing-pieces) flail out at the Prince like grotesque arms

Goblins rush in and surround the Prince who drives them back. A moving tree comes on to the stage wielding one bough like a club, and is also driven back. Finally, the Dragon enters breathing fire

The Prince defeats him, but sinks exhausted to the ground

The Dragon exits, mortally wounded

Prince	I'm finished but at least I've played my part.
	I lose but with an undefeated heart.
	Come, Comrade Death, and point the peaceful way,
	I've saved my honour, though I've lost the day!

Luna enters

Luna	Brave Prince, do not despair, success is near,
	Your troubles are about to disappear.
Prince	Most radiant fairy!
Luna	Take this golden key —

Act II, Scene 3   45

>   By it Malevola's powers will quickly flee.
>   And you must wear, to guard you in your task
>   And 'scape the sleeping curse — this charmèd mask.

The Prince takes the key and dons the mask which resembles that of Harlequin's, but with some "Fairy" glitter

	The key will ope' the silent palace gate,
	Within the Sleeping Beauty lies in state.
Prince	The Sleeping Beauty! This indeed is bliss.
Luna	Forward! and wake her with a lover's kiss.

Music: Tchaikovsky's "None But the Lonely Heart"

The Prince exits to one side of the Palace. Behind the palace gauze the Princess is revealed asleep on her bed. The Prince enters from one side

He approaches the bed, leans over and kisses the Princess. She wakes and gazes into the eyes of the Prince

Princess	Ah! What was that? Where am I? Who goes there?
	Why, somebody has kissed me, I declare!
	Is this the Prince, at last, my lips who pressed?
Prince	Oh course it was. (*He kisses her again*)
	There! You know all the rest.
	You are not angry at what I have done?
Princess	What, angry? No! My best thanks you have won.

The music for Song 9 begins

	How came you, sir, across the forest high?
Prince	To tell the truth, your highness, from the sky!

The Princess and Prince sing

Song 9

They dance together and the Lights slowly fade

Scene 4

The Palace of the New Republic

A modernized version of Act I, Scene 2. Everything and everybody, except the awakened sleepers, should be very futuristic in the Jules Verne manner — i.e. the future as the Victorians might have imagined it to be (see "Victorian Inventions" by Leonard de Vries [John Murray], etc.)

Obadiah I and Dogsbody enter

Dogsbody The place is altered since we last were here.
Obadiah I The court is altered too I greatly fear.

Four Senators enter on wheels with electric light bulbs on the top of their heads

Dogsbody Oh Lord! How curiously these people gaze!
Obadiah I No doubt your looks is strange — as is your ways.
Dogsbody Of course, they wonder very greatly who we are.
            You tell them!
Obadiah I   Oh, no! You. That's better far.
Dogsbody Good folks! We are not mad. We speak the truth;
            Although we seemingly retain our youth,
            We've been asleep for quite one hundred years.
1st Senator Ha!
2nd Senator   Ha!
3rd Senator   Ha!
4th Senator   Ha!
Obadiah I   What mean they by these jeers?

A loud gong is heard off stage

Senators The President!
Dogsbody   The President? Who's he?
1st Senator Be quiet, sir!
2nd Senator   And you —
3rd Senator   will quickly —
4th Senator   see!

Act II, Scene 4

The President enters on a pogo stick, with Guards in attendance

President Who are zese people? I do not know zese peoples! Why are zese people here when I do not know zem?
Dogsbody General Dogsbody, sir. Royal Equerry to His Majesty the King!
President I do not know zis Royal aquarium! Sounds fishy to me!
1st Senator Ha!
2nd Senator Ha!
3rd Senator Ha!
4th Senator Ha!
Dogsbody The lawful rulers of this country are the King and Queen of the Royal House of Prapsburg.
1st Senator No!
2nd Senator No!
3rd Senator No!
4th Senator No!
President Ah! My friend has been reading ze old legend. More zan one hundred years ago ze King and Queen disappeared wiz all zeir court — pouf! A great forest sprang up, and zere was no more King or Queen. Zere was no more Republic in ze Transvaal when Mistare Kruger disappeared, so zere is now no more kingdom in zis country. We are ze New Republic, and I am ze President — me!
Senators } *(together)* He!!
Guards
Dogsbody It's a lie! Long live the King! Long live the Queen!
President Is he mad? Arrest zem! Remove zer boots and put zem in chains!

The Guards start to carry off Dogsbody and Obadiah I

Obadiah I want to die with me boots on! I gotta die with me boots on! *Please* let me die with me boots on!
Senator Why do you want to die with your boots on?
Obadiah *(as he goes)* I got a hole in me sock!

The Guards, Dogsbody and Obadiah I exit

President So we deal wiz our enemies!

1st Senator *(applauding)* Bravo!
2nd Senator Bravo!
3rd Senator Bravo!
4th Senator Bravo!
President Ze old-fashioned fools wiz zeir old-fashioned ways! Here, everyzing is of ze latest invention!

The telephone rings. The 1st Senator hands it to the President

1st Senator Here, Excellency!
2nd Senator A call —
3rd Senator for you —
4th Senator on the telephonic machine!
President Hallo? ... Of course, dear. ... Zat's good. ... Zat's good. ... Zat's bad. ... Zat's good. ... Zat's good ... good ... good ... Oh, zat's bad. ... Good. ... Good! ... Good! *(He returns the telephone to Senator)*
Senator Who was it, Excellency?
President My wife. I was helping her choose ze strawberries. Whose is zat bag?
4th Senator *(picking up the Nurse's bag)* This one, Excellency?

The audience shouts

The Nurse enters and snatches the bag from the Senator

Nurse How dare you, sir! How dare you interfere with me reticule! *(She pushes the Senator away)*
Senator Here! Who do you think you're pushing?
Nurse I've no idea. What's your name?

She pushes him again into the other Senators, who all fall into a heap

President Who is ziz madwoman? Hey, you!
Nurse Don't you call me "You"! I don't mind being called "Hey" or "say there" or even "Pssst" But don't you dare call me "YOU"!
President Who are you, madam?
Nurse I think I must be the oldest inhabitant.
President How old are you?
Nurse *(coyly)* I shall be one hundred and twenty-one years old next week!

Act II, Scene 4

President One hundred and twenty-one?
Nurse Yes, but they tell me I still have the face of a young girl of seventeen!
President Well you'd better give it back, you're wrinkling it! Some lunatic asylum has broken loose, zat's evident.
Nurse Of course, that must be it! Tell me, sir, are you the Headkeeper?
President Keeper? I am ze President — me!
Senators
Guards } (*together*) He!!
Nurse Of the asylum?
President Of ze Republic!
Nurse Republic?
President Ze Grand Republic of Prapsburg!
Nurse Oh, the villains! Treason! I'll have you all gelatined. Long live the King!
President Arrest her too! In the name of Communism!

The Nurse is seized

Nurse Oh, Communism. I used to be a Communist.
President You?!
Nurse Yes. I began with Communism, drifted into Buddhism, and ended up with rheumatism!
President Away wiz her.
Nurse Unhand me, ruffians. In the name of Justice.
President Justice, madam? I am ze only Justice here!
Nurse In that case you should not only be done — you should be seen to be done!

The Nurse is carried off

Let go of me. Take that! Oooh! Long live the King! (*Etc., etc.*)

The Nurse exits with Guards

President So we deal wiz our enemies. I am ze President of ze New Republic — me!
Senators
Guards } (*together*) He!!

There is a gong heard off stage

Herald's voice (*through a large electric megaphone*) Miss Princess Beauty!

Music: Song 5

  The Princess enters

They all stare at her

Princess   Where is your etiquette? You can't do less
               Than welcome loyally your lost Princess.
1st Senator Oh!
2nd Senator   What a —
3rd Senator   charming —
4th Senator   girl!
President (*rolling his eyes lustily*) Stand back zere! I am ze President, and it is ze privilege of ze President to wait on beauty!
Princess Yes, sir, that is my name, but I don't know you!
President I am ze President of ze Grand Republic — me!
Princess Then what of my father — the King?
President Oh no! Not anozer of zem! What a pity! So young and so beautiful!

There is the sound of a gong off stage

Herald's voice (*through megaphone*) Mr Prince Florizel of Arcadia!
Princess Ah! here comes one who will tell you if I speak the truth or not.

  The Prince enters

Prince   At last I come to claim you as my bride,
            And never more be parted from your side.
            Through life I'll be your own true, faithful knight,
            Who hopes to find sweet favour in your sight.
Princess But tell me, Prince, the reason of this change,
            Why everything around me here is strange.
            This is the Royal Palace — where's the King?
            And where's Mamma? It's most astonishing.
            Who are these people round me here I see?

Act II, Scene 4   51

President I am ze President of ze Republic — me!
Senators ⎫
Guards ⎬ (*together*) He!!
Prince That's true. But though abolished is the throne,
                  The King and Queen return to claim their own!

There is the sound of a gong off stage

Herald's voice (*through megaphone*) Mr and Mrs King!

The King and Queen enter. The King carries his sceptre

The President, Senators and Attendants laugh

1st Senator Ha!
2nd Senator Ha!
3rd Senator Ha!
4th Senator Ha!
President Ha!
Queen They seem to find us funny. Have you got any of your clothes on inside out again?
King Certainly not! Look here, you people! I'm the King round here. (*He flourishes his sceptre*) And look there! There's me little wigger-wagger to prove it!

Song 10

The King sings the first verse and chorus and then everyone joins him for the subsequent choruses

President (*speaking*) Zo, you are ze king you zink.
King I am.
President And zis is your most interesting wife?
King This is my only wife!
Queen Certainly I'm his wife! You don't think I'd be living in sin with a face like that! I've given him the seventeen best years of my life.
King My goodness, were they your best?
President I am ze President of ze Republic — me! (*He snatches the sceptre away from the King*) I rule zis country!

The Queen faints

King You do? Then where do the King and Queen come in?
President Zey do not come in, zey go out!
Princess How dare you insult the mother who bore me.
President Yes — she bores me too.
King You might at least let us have the crown jewels to get a bit on.
President Ze crown jewels belong to ze nation, and are safely kept in the National Museum.
King Well soak my sennapods! That settles it. We're broke!
Princess Cheer up, Papa! Always remember — faith can move mountains.
King She must be a big strong girl!
Prince Fear not, your majesty! Do not despair.
     I'll soon be married to your daughter fair.
     And shall a prince e'er grudge his darling wife
     Her parents' comfort in her parents' life?
King I don't want to hurry you, my boy, but if our allowance dates from the day you get married, we'd like to know when it's coming off!
President I am ze President — me — as you know;
     I can divorce, and marry too also!
     And, if you would be married, why then, please
     Be married here, and I shall get me fees!
Prince Agreed?
Princess   Agreed!
President   Release the pris'ners now,
     That they may witness too the marriage vow!
     We'll celebrate. (*To the King*) Drink?
King No thank you!
President Cigar?
King No thank you!
President Turnip?
King I don't mind if I do!
President (*handing the King a turnip*) Follow me!

Music: Song 10

They all march off to the music

Obadiah I creeps on from the opposite side. He leads Frivolette by the hand. She wears ballet shoes, he wears clogs

Obadiah Now tell me, missy, what tribe is you?
Frivolette *(frightfully posh)* My name is Frivolette.
Obadiah 'As you ever been in love, Frivolette?
Frivolette Not ecktually in, but I've hovered around the edges. And what do they call you, pray?
Obadiah Obadiah.
Frivolette And *what* are you? Animal or vegetable?
Obadiah *(beaming at her lasciviously)* Ahhhrr!
Frivolette Animal!
Obadiah I be a famous blacksmith.
Frivolette A famous blacksmith? What are you famous for?
Obadiah Shoein' flies!
Frivolette Shoeing flies? That's impossible.
Obadiah Horse flies? Oh, Frivolette, you know that you've glad-eyed me. So now be nice, and come and sit beside me.

They sit

Now I'll show you what true love really is. Take hold my hand.
Frivolette Yes?
Obadiah Gaze into ma eyes.
Frivolette Yes.
Obadiah What do you see?
Frivolette Eyeballs!
Obadiah Keep gazin'. Does you feel you'se gettin' sozzely?
Frivolette Yes.
Obadiah Think!
Frivolette Yes.
Obadiah Has you thunk?
Frivolette Yes.
Obadiah Take away the number you first thought of.
Frivolette Yes.
Obadiah Swallow a big lump.
Frivolette Yes.
Obadiah Now then, both together, sigh —
Frivolette Yes ...

They both sigh

Obadiah That's love!

Obadiah I and Frivolette sing

Song 11

The traverse curtains close behind them as they dance: she on point, he a clog-dance. They reprise

They exit at the end of the song

SCENE 5

Outside the National Museum

A Guard enters as the scene changes. He takes a swig at his hipflask, spots the Nurse's bag, and goes to pick it up. The audience shouts. The Guard flees

There are motor-car noises off: backfiring, explosions, etc. The motor engine grinds to a halt. Silence

The Nurse enters, followed by the King

Nurse (*tragically*) This can't go on! This can't go on! This can't go on!
King What can't go on?
Nurse (*producing a tiny Wellington boot*) Beauty's Wellington boot. She's grown out of it!
King Never mind that. We're here. Look! There's the museum. Where are Beauty and the Prince?
Nurse They're our getaway people. They're standing guard over the motor car. New fangled contraptions!

Another explosion, off

King Ah, but it's the only truly democratic way to travel.
Nurse Motor cars? Democratic?
King Driving by the people, through the people, and over the people.
Nurse Well, come on then, your majesty, we'd better get on with it.
King I'm not at all sure about this lark, you know. I'm not cut out to be a burglar.

Act II, Scene 5

Nurse Oh, don't be silly, it's not burglary. The crown jewels are yours and you've a perfect right to take them!
King Well, I've never done anything like this before. I'd better take notes. (*He takes out a notebook and pencil*) I wonder which room they keep them in.
Nurse We'll enquire. But we'd better disguise ourselves first.

They put on masks and disguise themselves as burglars

(*Knocking on the door*) Hello there! Anyone at home?

A Curator enters from one side, making for the door

Look out! Excuse me, sir, are you the Curator of this museum?
Curator Yes, ma'am.
Nurse (*to the King*) Make a note of that. (*To the Curator*) I believe you have the crown jewels inside there.
Curator Yes, ma'am.
Nurse Got that down?
King Yes!
Nurse (*to the Curator*) Now, in which room are the jewels kept?
Curator That one!
Nurse (*to the King*) Crown jewels in room first elevation, left on plan. Note. One ladder! (*To the Curator*) Now tell me, is there anybody in the museum to take care of it?
Curator Only me, ma'am.
King (*writing*) "Only him."
Nurse And if you went away again, there wouldn't be anybody left?
Curator Nobody, ma'am!
King "Nobody."
Nurse Right! (*To the King*) Lend us yer shillelagh! (*She takes his sceptre. To the Curator*) Tell me, can you see any policemen about?
Curator No, ma'am.
Nurse Are you sure?
Curator Yes, ma'am.
Nurse Good.

She hits the Curator over the head with the sceptre. They catch him and dump him behind the wing-flat. They rush to the museum door and push with all their might. It won't budge

Nurse It's no good. Let's have a look at the plan.
King (*consulting the plan*) Look here, if you were to go round to the back, climb on the dog-kennel, from the dog-kennel to the water-butt, from there to the cistern, and then through the pigeon-loft on to the roof, you would ——
Nurse Fall off and break me bloomin' neck. I've got a better idea.
King What's that?
Nurse Give us a bunk up! (*She gets on to the King's shoulders*)

A Guard enters

Look out!

The Nurse hastily drops her skirts over the King's head. He gathers his long robes about him, so that they look like one gigantic nurse eleven feet high. The Guard takes another swig at his flask, and approaches the bag. The audience shouts. The Guard sees the Nurse, gapes in horror, looks at his flask accusingly and flings it away. The Nurse/King chase him round the stage and off, swinging at him with the sceptre

The Guard exits

The Nurse stands on the King's shoulders and enters the museum window

(*At the window*) Call the prince. Tell him to stand by with the motor car.

The Nurse disappears

The King whistles to the Prince and waves him on. There is a loud explosion, off

The Prince, driving, with the Princess pushing, enter with the motor car which grinds to a halt, c, after a final bang

Princess Couldn't we just walk there?
Prince No! No! It's quicker by car. (*He gets out, raises the bonnet and peers in and fiddles with the engine during the following*)
King (*over the Prince's shoulder*) Perhaps it needs a new flint.
Princess Did you remember to trim the wick?

Act II, Scene 5

The Nurse appears at the window

Nurse Below there! (*She throws out a sack containing the crown jewels*)

The Nurse disappears

King (*inspecting the contents of the sack*) Let's see if we've got everything. Yes, here's my summer crown with the ventilator on the roof, and here's my winter crown with fur round the edges.

A moth flies out and the King swipes at it with his sceptre

The Nurse enters through the door — it opens outwards

Nurse Here we are, then.
King How did you get the door open?
Nurse It opens outwards!
Princess (*to the Prince*) What on earth's the matter with the thing?
Prince It's jibbed.
Princess (*fingers in ears*) I hope it isn't going to back jump!
Prince (*in the driver's seat*) Will you turn the handle, please?
Nurse Which handle?
King That one.
Nurse Which way do I turn it?
Prince Turn it this way, and then if nothing happens turn it the other way.
Nurse Right!

Explosion! The handle throws the Nurse through the air. The car gives a loud burp

King Manners! I wonder why it did that?
Princess Papa. You'd better get under and have a look. Here's the book of instructions.
King (*climbing under the car*) Me? Why does it have to be me?
All It's your car!

Nuts enters and goes to the car

King Pass me the spanner, will you?

Nuts hands him the spanner, then goes to the rear of the car and lets the tyre down. There is a loud hissing

  Nuts exits

There is a puff of smoke from the car engine

Nurse Now what have you done?
King Won't be long now.

Song 12

The Prince and Princess sing

The song continues during the following: the King and Nurse emerge from tinkering with the engine, discover the flat rear tyre, take out the pump, and pump up the tyre

  Nuts enters and lets down the front tyre

The Prince and the Princess discover the flat front tyre, take the pump and pump up the tyre while the King and Nurse continue singing

All four pump up the tyre, and then climb into the car as they sing

Explosion! The back of the car gives way and the King and Nurse tumble out. The Prince and the Princess climb out to help the King and Nurse to their feet

  Nuts climbs into the driving seat and exits in the car

King (*speaking*) I don't know what to make of that dog.
Nurse Have you thought of a rug?
Voices (*off*) Down with the President! Down with the President!

  A Guard enters

All Four Oh-oh!
King It's a fair cop!

Act II, Scene 5

Prince All right, Constable, we'll come quietly.
Nurse (*indicating crowd noises off*) What's all the to-do?
Guard The President has imposed an unpopular tax on the people.
King A tax? On what?
Guard On bicycles.
Prince Then we've got a chance, by George! No government can tax bicycles here and hope to remain in power.
Guard There is much discontent and whispers of a revolution.
Nurse A revolution. Good. The monarchy will be restored.
Princess And you will be king once more, dear Papa.
Guard That's what all the people are saying.
All Hooray!

The Crowd (every available character, some pushing period bicycles) enter, led by Dogsbody wearing a "Keir Hardy" cloth cap, and riding a penny-farthing bicycle, followed by the Queen, Frivolette, Obadiah, etc.

Crowd Down with the President! Down with the President!
King Down with the President!
Dogsbody Long live Mr and Mrs King!
All Long live Mr and Mrs King!
Princess Mama! I do believe you are behind all this!
Queen Not at all. It was Dogsbody, the dear man.
Dogsbody Up the revolution!
All Up the revolution!
Princess Well, Mama, I'm to be married, so there!
Queen Oooooooh! (*She faints into Dogsbody's arms*)

The President enters, guarded

There are angry murmurs from the crowd

King Who's this coming?
Prince It is ze President of the Grand Republic — he!
All He!!
President Alas, no sir, I am deposed. But tomorrow I leave for ze continent. I am going to become a monk and amaze all my enemies. (I haven't got any friends.) I shall become a monk and *drown* myself in Benedictine!

Queen (*reviving*) Have you got the crown jewels, Henry?
King Here, my love. There's yours and here's mine. But most important of all, everybody, look! What's this?
All It's the little wigger-wagger in his hand!

Song 13

The Princess, Dogsbody, the Nurse, King, Obadiah I and Frivolette sing the words of the chorus in turn

The Stage Manager enters with the words

Everyone joins in a repeat of the chorus

Everyone, except the King and Nurse, exits at the end of the song

Song 13 becomes the house number

Nurse Didn't they sing that well?
King They certainly did.
Nurse But I'll tell you one thing. The girls sang it much louder than the boys.
King Oh no they didn't! (*Etc., etc.*)

Ad lib with the audience

Let's have a competition! (*Etc., etc.*)

They ad lib. The audience competes in singing the song

Scene 6

The Abode of Time

Malevola enters

Malevola Yet of me deep revenge they'll have a taste,
For I, Malevola, their lives shall waste!

Father Time enters

Act II, Scene 6

Time Avaunt, vile craven! You, the goblins' minion,
Remember you're once more in *my* dominion.
Behave yourself! As for the royal pair,
So sweet a couple we'll preserve with care.

Malevola May neither let the other have their way!
Each night be more unhappy than the day!
Their wedded bliss be blighted with frustrations.
They'll not enjoy their marital relations.
Connubially they'll both be incomplete,
No patter shall there be of tiny feet!
My malefaction both of them pursue
With every day some evil — sad and new!

Luna enters

Luna So you are at it still! But all in vain —
You'd threaten vengeance — but I'm here again.
Malevola, you've lost. Pride's had its fall!
The mills of Time still grind exceeding small.
Virtuous powers must triumph in the end!
Repent. Return. We want you back, old friend.
Your peers shall welcome you in Fairyland.
(She extends her hand)

Malevola *(touching Luna's fingertips with her own)*
Is it true? Such mercy is beyond belief!

Time Your earthly record's gone. I'll burn each leaf:
Bygones are bygones, I've wiped out the past,
Luna, Malevola — be friends at last!

Malevola *(restraining her tears)*
Oh, joy!

Luna Now we must journey where my wand
Shall show once more the powers of Fairyland.

She produces two invitation cards, one of which she gives to Malevola, who clutches it to herself with delight

We're both invited, now, to do our duty
At the Wedding of our Godchild — Sleeping Beauty!

Song 14: Everyone Loves a Fairy When She's Forty!
(to the tune of **Nobody Loves a Fairy When She's Forty!**
by Arthur Le Clerq)

Luna	Ev'ryone loves a fairy when she's forty,
	Ev'ryone loves a fairy when she's old.
	To say she's lost her magic power's a lot of tarradiddle!
Malevola (*brightening*)	
	There's many a lively melody played on an older fiddle!
Luna	Age cannot wither *her*, nor custom stale her,
	Though her hair looks more like rust instead of gold.
Malevola	Each goblin and each pixie
	Knows she still can turn quite tricksey!
Both	Ev'ryone loves a fairy when she's old!

They dance in a very stately manner. Finally:

> Age cannot wither *her*, nor custom stale her,
> Though her hair looks more like rust instead of gold.
> They'll all be shouting "What O!"
> Ev'ry time they pass her grotto.
> Ev'ryone loves a fairy, ev'ryone loves a fairy,
> Ev'ryone loves a fairy,
> When she's old!

They exit

Scene 7

The Palace

The Princess's wedding. Walk-down

Music. The Guests are dancing. They finish, bow to each other, then to the audience

The principals walk down to "Work, Boys, Work!"

Act II, Scene 7

King	Give me your hand, my brave, my noble son,
	We glory in the deed that you have done.
Prince	This lovely maiden's right I freely own
	To share in my succession and my throne.
Princess	Great Sovereign, it is most nobly said,
	But you must know your daughter fair hath wed
	No pauper prince. He brings you worth untold,
	Your coffers will soon be well filled with gold!

Nuts spies the Nurse's bag and picks it up. The audience shout. The Nurse snatches it away from Nuts

Nurse Here you are, love. I've been meaning to give you this for years, hundreds of years! It's your christening present. What with one thing and another I never got round to it. There!

She takes out a pair of baby's rompers and a rattle. Everyone laughs. The Princess blushes

Oh well, never mind. They'll come in very handy later on!

The Stage Manager enters with the words to Song 13

The Nurse conducts with the rattle as they sing the final chorus

Song 15 (reprise of Song 13)

CURTAIN

FURNITURE AND PROPERTY LIST

ACT I
Scene 1

On stage: Huge rock. *On it*: huge hour-glass

Personal: **Malevola**: chains, wand (used throughout)

Scene 2

On stage: Two thrones

Off stage: Large tray containing a stethoscope, town crier's hat, bowler hat, General's helmet, top hat, admiral's cocked hat (**Frivolette**)
Baby (**Nurse**)
Crib, feeding bottle, powder puff, nappy, gold stool (**Maids**)
Nurse's bag containing rubber squeaky Guinness bottle, parcel, pair of baby's rompers and rattle (**Maid**)
Easel and placard with chorus lyrics for Song (**Stage Manager**)
Sceptre (**King**)
Casket (**Luna**)
Rose (**Vedonia**)
Chain of precious stones (**Elegantia**)
Silver fairy bells (**Melodia**)
Golden ballet shoes (**Camilla**)
Golden chalice (**Thalia**)
Laurel wreath (**Pamela**)

Personal: **Luna**: wand (used throughout)

Sleeping Beauty

Scene 3

On stage: Large trick hour-glass/tea-table with cups, saucers, cakes, etc.
Big clock with movable hand

Off stage: Scythe (**Father Time**)

Scene 4

On stage: Ironing board, iron, clothes
Washing line with pegs and washing
Scrubbing brush, pail
Brooms, etc.
Half-crown (for **King**)
Spinning wheels upstage behind gauze
Golden spinning wheel behind wall upstage

Off stage: Bags on tray (**Street Vendor**)
Schoolbooks (**Nurse**)
Pedlar's tray (**Malevola**)

Set: Princess's bed behind gauze

Personal: **Malevola**: key

Scene 5

On stage: Large trick hour-glass as before
Big clock with movable hand

Off stage: Scythe (**Time**)

Scene 6

On stage: Two axes (for **Obadiah I and II**)
Three bags, one containing pomegranates
Jules Verne-type flying machine behind gauze

Off stage: Balloon basket with deflating balloon (**Stage Management**)
Song lyrics on placard (**Stage Manager**)

Personal: **Prince**: goggles

ACT II
SCENE 1

On stage: Large trick hour-glass as before
Big clock with movable hand
Flowers, plants, etc. (for **Father Time**)

SCENE 2

On stage: Bed upstage behind gauzes

Off stage: Bouquet (**Nurse**)
Song 8 lyrics on placard (**Stage Manager**)

SCENE 2A

Off stage: Magic bat (**Harlequin**)
Handcart with various joints of meat, poultry, rabbits, large black pudding, sausages, long knife sharpener, baby bottle, etc. (**Butcher**)
Truncheon (**Policeman**)
Stick (**Pantaloon**)
Baby in large pram with baby bottle (**Nursemaid**)
Butterfly net (**Clown**)

Personal: **Policeman**: whistle
Butcher: cardboard heart cut-out in breast pocket

SCENE 3

On stage: Bed upstage behind gauze

Sleeping Beauty

Scene 4

On stage: Telephone

Off stage: Pogo stick (**President**)
Sceptre (**King**)

Personal: **President**: turnip

Scene 5

On stage: Museum cut-out with practical door

Off stage: Sceptre (**King**)
Motor car with instructions, spanner, pump (**Prince, Princess**)
Sack containing jewels (**Nurse**)
Penny-farthing (**Dogsbody**)
Period bicycles (**Crowd**)
Song 13 lyrics on placard (**Stage Manager**)

Personal: **Guard**: hip flask
Nurse: tiny Wellington boot, mask
King: mask, pencil, notebook

Scene 6

On stage: Large trick hour-glass as before

Off stage: Scythe (**Time**)

Personal: **Luna**: two invitation cards

Scene 7

On stage: Nil

Off stage: Lyrics to Song 13 on placard (**Stage Manager**)

LIGHTING PLOT

ACT I, SCENE 1

To open: Lightning, fiery effect on rock, dim lighting downstage

Cue 1	**Malevola's chains break asunder** *Harvest moon effect*	(Page 2)
Cue 2	**Malevola and Luna disappear** *Lightning*	(Page 3)

ACT I, SCENE 2

To open: Full general lighting

Cue 3	**Luna: "... your sweet babe's defence."** *Lightning, lights fade up and down*	(Page 9)

No cues

ACT I, Scene 3

To open: General lighting

Cue 4	**Time: "... sixteen years ago!"** *Lighting whirls*	(Page 13)

ACT I, Scene 4

To open: General lighting

Cue 5	**Nurse: "... as they do the measles."** *Lighting begins to dim*	(Page 19)

Cue 6	**Princess:** " ... in my dreams." *Bring up lighting behind gauze*	(Page 19)
Cue 7	At the end of Song 5 *Fade lighting behind gauze*	(Page 19)
Cue 8	**Malevola** enters *Green spot on* **Malevola**	(Page 20)
Cue 9	The **Nurse** opens the door and enters *Bring up lighting behind gauze*	(Page 21)
Cue 10	The **Nurse** exits *Fade lighting behind gauze*	(Page 21)
Cue 11	**Malevola** exits *Fade green spot*	(Page 21)
Cue 12	**Princess Beauty** exits *Darken lighting; when ready, bring up lighting behind gauze*	(Page 21)
Cue 13	**Princess:** "Mamma! Papa!" *Fade lighting upstage behind gauze*	(Page 24)
Cue 14	**Luna:** "... we can exchange a doze." *Bring up lighting behind gauze*	(Page 25)

ACT I, Scene 5

To open: Whirling light effect

Cue 15	**Time:** "The star of hope is born!" *Star lights up*	(Page 27)
Cue 16	**Chorus of voices:** "Old Father Time!" *Fade to black-out*	(Page 27)

ACT I, Scene 6

To open: Lighting downstage

Cue 17	**Luna** points her wand to first gauze *Bring up lighting behind gauze*	(Page 32)

ACT II, Scene 1

To open: General lighting

No cues

ACT II, Scene 2

To open: General lighting downstage

Cue 18	As **Luna** speaks *Bring up lighting upstage on* **Princess** *behind gauze*	(Page 37)

ACT II, Scene 2A

To open: Lighting upstage behind gauze

Cue 19	When ready *Follow spot on* **Harlequin**	(Page 37)
Cue 20	**Beauty** goes to **Harlequin** *Bring up general lighting*	(Page 37)
Cue 21	**Harlequin** and **Colombine** stand triumphant *Black-out; spot on* **Malevola**	(Page 42)

ACT II, Scene 3

To open: Lighting downstage

Cue 22	The **Prince** exits to one side of the palace *Bring up lighting upstage behind gauze*	(Page 45)
Cue 23	The **Prince** and **Princess** dance together *Fade to black-out*	(Page 45)

ACT II, Scene 4

To open: Full general lighting

No cues

ACT II, Scene 5

To open: General lighting

No cues

ACT II, Scene 6

To open: General lighting

No cues

ACT II, Scene 7

To open: General lighting

No cues

EFFECTS PLOT

ACT I

Cue 1	To open *Music "Walpurgisnacht" by Gounod; thunder*	(Page 1)
Cue 2	Last grain drops into the hour-glass *Spark, small puff of smoke; roll of thunder; large flash, puff of smoke*	(Page 2)
Cue 3	**Malevola** and **Luna** disappear *Thunder*	(Page 3)
Cue 4	The girls crowd round and kiss **Dogsbody** *Fanfare*	(Page 3)
Cue 5	**Lackey**: " ... the Princess Beauty!" *Music: royal march*	(Page 4)
Cue 6	**Dogsbody** exits followed by **Frivolette** *Baby howls*	(Page 4)
Cue 7	**Nurse** chases the **Lackey** round the stage *Loud fanfare*	(Page 6)
Cue 8	**Lackey**: "... the King and Queen!" *Music: regal march*	(Page 6)
Cue 9	**King**: " ... and the kettledrum!" *Flourish. Music*	(Page 7)
Cue 10	**Luna**: "... your sweet babe's defence." *Thunder*	(Page 9)

Sleeping Beauty

Cue 11	To open Scene 3 *Fade in sound of hundreds of ticking clocks, loud peal of electric bells*	(Page 12)
Cue 12	**Time:** " ... sixteen years ago!" *Hundreds of different clock chimes and bells*	(Page 13)
Cue 13	**Malevola** enters *Hiss of cymbals*	(Page 20)
Cue 14	**Princess Beauty** enters *Music: "Gretchen Am Spinnrade" by Franz Schubert*	(Page 21)
Cue 15	To open Scene 5 *Hundreds of ticking clocks, church bells gently tolling*	(Page 27)
Cue 16	**Time:** "Ding-dong! Ding-dong!" *Distant church bells*	(Page 27)
Cue 17	**Obadiah I** strikes **Obadiah II** with the axe handle *Sound effect*	(Page 28)
Cue 18	**Obadiah II** scoops the pomegranates into the bag *Rumbling; distant hiss of escaping air*	(Page 29)
Cue 19	**Prince's voice:** (4th time) "Ahoy! Ahoy!" *Violent hiss of air from above; music: descending arpeggios*	(Page 30)
Cue 20	**Luna:** " ... our tale to end." *Violent hiss of air, music: rising arpeggios; dry ice*	(Page 32)

ACT II

Cue 21	To open Scene 1 *Music background*	(Page 34)
Cue 22	**Malevola:** " ... is both big and strong..." *Fearful roar*	(Page 35)

Cue 23	**Malevola:** " ... all of mortal mould." *Roar*	(Page 35)
Cue 24	**Malevola:** " ... so adieu!" *Flash*	(Page 35)
Cue 25	Everyone exits at the end of Song 8 *Music as script: "Beautiful Galathea" by Franz von Suppé*	(Page 36)
Cue 26	**Malevola** exits. The Dragon enters *Sound of approaching airship*	(Page 43)
Cue 27	The Dragon retreats *Airship descends*	(Page 43)
Cue 28	**Obadiah I:** " ... from the skies!" *Dragon roars*	(Page 43)
Cue 29	**Malevola** enters and speaks *Drum roll*	(Page 43)
Cue 30	**Malevola** exits *Music*	(Page 44)
Cue 31	**Luna:** " ... and wake her with a lover's kiss." *Music: Tchaikovsky's "None But the Lonely Heart"*	(Page 45)
Cue 32	**Obadiah I:** "What mean they by these jeers?" *Loud gong*	(Page 46)
Cue 33	**President:** " ... ze latest invention!" *Telephone*	(Page 48)
Cue 34	**Senators** and **Guards:** "He!!" *Gong,* **Herald'***s voice through megaphone as script*	(Page 49)
Cue 35	**President:** " So young and so beautiful!" *Gong,* **Herald'***s voice through megaphone as script*	(Page 50)

Cue 36	**Prince:** " ... to claim their own!" *Gong,* **Herald'***s voice through megaphone as script*	(Page 51)
Cue 37	**The Guard** flees *Motor car sounds: backfiring, explosions etc., engine grinds to a halt*	(Page 54)
Cue 38	**Nurse:** "New fangled contraptions!" *Explosion*	(Page 54)
Cue 39	The **King** whistles to **Prince** and waves him on *Loud explosion; followed by explosion*	(Page 56)
Cue 40	**Nurse:** "Right!" *Explosion; car gives a loud burp*	(Page 57)
Cue 41	**Nuts** lets the tyre down *Loud hissing; followed by puff of smoke from car engine*	(Page 58)
Cue 42	All four climb into the car as they sing *Explosion*	(Page 58)

www.ingramcontent.com/pod-product-compliance
Ingram Content Group UK Ltd.
Pitfield, Milton Keynes, MK11 3LW, UK
UKHW021845210426
5322IPUK00022B/477